Diverse Voices, Challenging Injustice

Banner Tales from Glasgow

Edited by David Featherstone, Fiona Hayes,
Helen M Hughes and Isobel McDonald

First published in 2021 by the Scottish Labour History Society in association with Glasgow Museums and the University of Glasgow School of Geographical and Earth Sciences.

Text © individual contributors and institutions
Images © as noted in the text
Glasgow Museums photography by William Docherty, Jim Dunn, and Chris Jamieson
Original design and typography by Jay Bernard, additional design and typography by Jacqui Duffus
ISBN 978-1-9163050-0-7

Printed in England by Mixam UK Ltd.

Foreword

Stewart Maclennan, Chair, Scottish Labour History Society

Since its foundation in 1961, the Scottish Labour History Society has been a leading force in labour history in Scotland. Its membership of individual, organizational and academic subscribers coalesces with others to organize seminars, conferences, labour heritage activities and provide expert advice and practical support in the preservation and promotion of labour history.

Our annual peer-reviewed journal, *Scottish Labour History*, now in its fifty-fifth edition, attracts worldwide subscription. Recent initiatives have included a new website, www.scottishlabourhistorysociety.scot, and the development of a number of Occasional Publications (see the Further Resources section, p.104), of which *Diverse Voices, Challenging Injustice: Banner Tales from Glasgow* is the latest.

We are proud to play a part in telling the stories featured in this publication – all of which emerged during the lifetime of our Society – and to share that role with our partners at Glasgow Museums and the Human Geography Research Group, University of Glasgow. Readers can best honour the causes represented in *Diverse Voices, Challenging Injustice* with their active support.

Introduction

David Featherstone, Fiona Hayes, Helen M Hughes,
Isobel McDonald

This publication arose from *Banner Tales*, a collaborative project which has explored the banners of trade unions and political campaigns primarily in Glasgow. Trade union banners have long been recognized as a central part of the symbolic and material culture of the labour movement. Integral to the ways movements assert their presence, the slogans and images on banners also crystallize the values and aspirations of these movements and campaigns.[1] Here, discussions of banners and the organizing cultures they were part of are used to engage with experiences of the peace movement, the ways in which Glaswegians of South Asian heritage have experienced and contributed to the labour movement, and the relations between Glasgow and the anti-apartheid movement. Drawing on *Banner Tales* workshops on these themes held between 2016 and 2018, this book brings together eight testimonies and interviews along with images of banners linked to these movements. Through doing so it offers a distinctive and original lens on diverse forms of organizing in Scotland against injustices and oppression.

Glasgow Museums holds a significant collection of trade union and other banners, and this publication builds on collaborations developed in relation to the collection. The *Banner Tales* project has used these banners to engage with different aspects of the recent histories of organizing in Glasgow. The project was the result of a partnership initiated in 2013 by Johnnie Crossan, then a PhD student working on social movements in Glasgow, later a researcher on the Banners project, between geographers from the University of Glasgow with a strong interest in labour and social movements and Glasgow Museums staff who were keen to engage local communities in exploring and recording the significance and history of the banners and the context of their use. Richard Leonard, then GMB Regional Political Officer, and later leader of the Scottish Labour Party (2017–2021), was involved in the original stages of the project and was invaluable in sourcing contacts from the broader labour movement. In 2015 we organized a series of workshops which were based on taking banners out of the museum stores to community venues in their places of origin across Glasgow. We displayed them alongside banners from local groups as the focal point for discussion, and invited activists involved in trade union and other forms of political organizing to talk about the banners and what they represent. We worked closely with local community groups and venues so that each event reflected activism, past and present, in that area.

...RITAIN SPENDS
...3 BILLION A YEAR
...N ARMAMENTS —
...6 PER FAMILY PER
...EEK — 14 TIMES
...HAT WE GIVE IN
...ERSEAS AID —
...UBLE TOTAL
...BLIC EXPEND-
...URE IN SCOTLAND

ONE TRIDENT MISSILE
COSTS THE EQUIVALENT
OF 100 HOSPITALS.
EACH TRIDENT SUB.
HAS THE DESTRUCTIVE
POWER OF ABOUT 200
HIROSHIMA BOMBS —
WHICH ITSELF KILLED
78,000 AND DES-
-TROYED AN ENTIRE
CITY.

SCOTLA...
HIGHEST
-TION O...
WEAPON...
COUNTRY...
BE A PRI...
NOWHER...
SAFE, A...
OF THE ...
CENTRA...
WOULD B...

**Detail of the posters displayed on the Peace March
Scotland 1982 bus.**
Image © and courtesy of Maggi Sale.

Participants at a *Banner Tales* event in Scotland Street School Museum, Glasgow.
Image © CSG CIC Glasgow Museums Collection.

This proved to be a very productive process. Testimonies from attendees at these workshops relating to both high-profile campaigns and disputes, as well as less well-known events such as the long-running Morris's furniture strike from the mid-1980s, were published in an earlier booklet.[2]

What we found particularly useful about these events was the ways in which engagement with the banners worked to spark discussion and to draw out diverse, often hidden, aspects of the work of labour organizing. By taking banners into community spaces we encouraged a set of discussions to emerge which brought different conversations and knowledge together. This reconnection with place gave the banners a new life, inspiring discussions that provided insights on past forms of political organizing as well as informing debates about current political activities in Glasgow and further afield. It helped value and validate these accounts. The outcomes of the workshops were both expected and unexpected; learning about the banners and political and labour organizing was expected, but the emotional response to the banners and the telling of personal histories related to the banners was unexpected and powerful. This emotional resonance was underlined by the inclusion of music at the *Banner Tales* events, revealing how both political songs and banners were integral parts of the culture of the labour movement. These events provided a format we used for the later workshops that are mentioned here.

The first section of the publication draws on a workshop on the theme of women peace campaigners, held at Glasgow Women's Library on 18 June 2016. The event marked the centenary of the founding of the Women's Peace Crusade in Glasgow, a movement initiated and run by women to bring World War I to an end. (The leaders of the Crusade had already been involved in running the successful Rent Strike campaign of 1915.) In line with such long histories of women's involvement in activism in relation to peace in Glasgow, the workshop included Paul Griffin's discussion of suffragette and feminist Helen Crawfurd's activist work which drew attention to her internationalism.[3] The other speaker was Maggi Sale, Convenor of the Peace March Scotland, a 33-day march from Inverness to Edinburgh during July and August 1982 organized by the Scottish Convention for Peace and Disarmament.

Sale's account (see pp.14–32) gives a vivid sense of the experience of both the march and the way its banner was used. It also clearly conveys the significant personal stress and impact of organizing the march. Her words provide an insight into the effects of activism at a personal level – the ending of relationships, the forging of new ones and changing perceptions. The primary purpose of the march was 'to inform and activate the people of Scotland in the cause of Peace'[4] and the banner, now in Glasgow Museums' collection, was integral to shaping the march's impact and bringing a disparate group of people together. Led by Buddhist monks, Scottish, Chilean and Japanese peace activists marched alongside the banner, reflecting the internationalism of movements for peace. The imagery of the Peace March banner articulated a hopeful opposition to the threat of nuclear war, drawing on a design by Sale's daughter Gwen.

Sale also gives a sense of how the march and the banners carried on it were shaped by the political context of mass unemployment and entrenched opposition to Thatcherism (the Conservative Party, led by Margaret Thatcher, was in power) at that time. She describes there being 'a hard core of 40 of them that walked' who were 'very sort of militant, unemployed workers and what have you. And all the banners that went with that'. This aspect of the march can be seen as part of the antagonistic political cultures which form a long-standing part of movements for peace in the west of Scotland, a tradition that goes back to the concerted opposition to the siting of US Polaris submarines at Holy Loch in the early 1960s.[5] Indeed, at one of the earlier *Banner Tales* workshops held in Barmulloch, in the north of Glasgow, in 2015, Bob Gillespie, now an 'old' Springburn Young Socialist, recounted how that organization's banner had been taken to the demonstration at Glasgow's Queen's Park on May Day 1962 when the 'Young Socialists walked out on Hugh Gaitskell during his speech. He was talking about nuclear weapons and he started haranguing the Young Socialists as "agents of Moscow".[6]

Suki Sangha, Chair of the Scottish Trades Union Congress (STUC) Black Workers' Committee between October 2017 and October 2018, observes that 'We don't always hear many stories about black and minority ethnic workers organizing in the trade unions'. The second section of the publication helps counter this absence. It draws on the *Banner Tales* workshop held in March 2017 which explored the ways in which Glaswegians of South Asian heritage have both experienced and contributed to the labour movement.

This event was linked to the *GaswegAsians* exhibition, 'a unique display located within Scotland Street School Museum [2017–2020] and developed in partnership with Colourful Heritage, an organization devoted to gathering and sharing experiences of South Asian immigration in Scotland'.[7] A small, square, textile printed 'Indian Workers Union Glasgow' was included in this exhibition and we were keen to find out more about this.[8] We used it as a way into the discussions at the workshop which featured Bob Chadha MBE, a former Labour councillor in Cumbernauld, speaking about his long experience of various forms of political organizing, and Suki Sangha speaking in relation to the STUC Black Workers' Committee banner.

Sangha's contribution positions the discussion in relation to the broader context of Black, Asian and Minority Ethnic (BAME) labour organizing. This sits alongside the edited texts of interviews by Glasgow Museums' curator Isobel McDonald, from the *GlaswegAsians* exhibition team, with Bob Chadha and Gurdev Singh Pall, who was involved in the Rail and Maritime Transport Union (RMT) during the 1990s and 2000s. These accounts give a sense of the longevity of forms of organizing by workers of South Asian heritage in Glasgow and the importance of their different trajectories and experiences. Gurdev Singh Pall describes the formation of a Glasgow branch of the Indian Workers' Association (IWA), established after Puran Singh Pall, together with a colleague, contacted the IWA in England and requested permission to establish a branch in Scotland. This permission was granted in 1971. The discussions of the IWA here are significant as they give a sense of the importance of that organization's role in Scotland and also indicate some of its key activities. These accounts enhance important existing work on the IWA which tends to focus on the numerically stronger movements in the West Midlands and Southall.[9]

Through Bob Chadha and Gurdev Singh Pall's testimonies, the IWA emerges as part of a terrain of organizing and engagement shaped by a number of organizations which often intersected with each other. Thus Chadha describes being involved in forms of organizing including multi-ethnic youth work, the Labour Party, the Scottish Co-operative Movement and the national and local government workers trade union NALGO. He shows how these aspects of his political engagement were integrated, and how they shaped multi-ethnic solidarities and institutions such as the United Youth Club. As with other recent testimonies of Scottish Asians in Glasgow, such as the collection edited by Gauri Raje and Churnjeet Mahn, these testimonies give an important sense of the multi-ethnic cultures of some unions in Glasgow, especially in relation to transport.[10]

Gurdev Singh Pall and Bob Chadha also highlight the tensions that could be present in such support and movements. It is clear that while at one level unions and the Labour Party were inclusive, there were barriers when BAME workers sought to get elected to positions. Gurdev Singh Pall and Bob Chadha's recollections underline the importance of Black/Asian Workers' committees, their roles in shaping them and their contrasting perspectives on them.[11] Such committees or sections, as Suki Sangha explains, were:

'initiated by Black and minority ethnic trade unionists and they were the ones that were actively involved in creating those structures and actually pushing down a lot of barriers that were put up. I suppose back then a lot of Black organizations seemed a threat, something the trade union movement couldn't control, then they were going to shut that down in any way possible and that's reflected in some of the stories that you hear from over the years.'

She also draws attention to the importance of recognizing diverse forms of organizing and solidarity, such as the Grunwick strike in London 1976–78 which gained significant support from the Scottish labour movement.[12]

The testimonies in this section give a strong sense of the impact of racism and the significance of attempts to challenge it. Bob Chadha recounts being involved in campaigns related to the IWA, such as the opposition to Peter Griffiths' racist election campaign in Smethwick in 1964, while he was based in Birmingham before moving to Glasgow. He also mentions the frightening impact of Enoch Powell's 'Rivers of Blood' speech in April 1968. The IWA, as Shirin Hirsch has stressed, was active in challenging both the speech itself and the racist violence that it catalyzed and legitimized.[13] Issues of racist violence are not, however, confined to this now relatively distant past. As Neil Davidson and Satnam Virdee have recently argued, 'racism remains a significant problem in Scottish society, irrespective of the other more progressive transformations that are currently on-going'.[14] Suki Sangha discusses encountering the labour movement following the racist murder of her uncle Surjit Singh Chhokar in 1998. She comments on the solidarity shaped by the physical presence of trade union banners on demonstrations, and signals the significance of the annual STUC anti-racist demonstration established in 1998 'by trade unionists in the STUC working together with the local Black community in Glasgow' to 'confront attempts by the BNP [British National Party] to take over St Andrew's Day'.[15] This remains the only annual anti-racist trade union demonstration in the UK.

A key way in which the Scottish labour movement has been involved in challenging racism has been in relation to internationalist struggles and solidarities. While opposition to apartheid is often now presented as having been a consensual political position, the anti-apartheid movement in Scotland, as Suganya Chetty's contribution here notes, faced significant opposition, which could be both racist and violent.[16] The final section features contributions by Suganya Chetty, Brian Filling and John Nelson, based on talks given at a *Banner Tales* event in October 2018 held in association with the Archive Centre at Glasgow Caledonian University (which holds the archives of the Scottish Committee of the Anti-Apartheid Movement)[17]. Discussion was prompted by Jim Cathcart's evocative 1981 banner 'Nelson Mandela – Freeman of Glasgow – Prisoner of Apartheid', created to mark the Freedom of the City award to Nelson Mandela, now part of Glasgow Caledonian University Archive Centre, and the banner of the Sechaba International Festival (held in Glasgow in 1990) from Glasgow Museums' collection.

The testimonies of Brian Filling and John Nelson, Chair and Secretary of the Scottish Committee of the Anti-Apartheid Movement respectively, give important insights into the campaigns which resulted in Mandela being made a Freeman of the City of Glasgow in 1981 while he was still imprisoned on Robben Island. They both provide a clear sense of the reconfiguring of place through these forms of internationalist politics and the sustained organization that it took to make Glasgow a city which was a significant force in challenging apartheid. As John Nelson explains, the fact that Glasgow was the first city to offer Mandela the honour of Freeman of the City did not 'come from nowhere'. Rather, as he emphasizes, it was the product of sustained organizing. Famously, the renaming of St George's Place (where the South African consulate was located) in 1986 as Nelson Mandela Place also speaks to the way the identity of the city, and what it stood for, was reworked through these struggles.[18] In his recent discussion of the relations between the Scottish anti-apartheid movement and the Scottish labour movement, Chris Fevre comments that this 'deeply embarrassed the South African government'.[19]

Filling's discussion of the ceremony where Mandela's Freeman-ship was accepted by Alex Ekwueme, the Nigerian Vice-President who had studied for a PhD at Glasgow's University of Strathclyde,[20] gives a sense of the particular internationalist connections which shaped this organizing. These connections also cross-cut Cold War geopolitics. Suganya Chetty argues that the Solidarity Committee of the German Democratic Republic was particularly instrumental in supporting the African National Congress (ANC). She also highlights the way anti-apartheid struggle and other forms of internationalism were part of the cultures of the Scottish labour movement with events such as Miners' galas and May Day rallies.[21] These events, as the images on pp.54–55 suggest (the banners of the Scottish Immigrant Labour Council and print union SOGAT), brought together organizations from across the labour movement in Scotland. The strong involvement of different trade unions and trade unionists in the Sechaba festival in 1990 also speaks to these connections and relations.

The Sechaba Festival was held in the year that Glasgow was European Capital of Culture. That it was subtitled 'cultural resistance to apartheid' underlines how the Capital of Culture was used as a political moment. As Filling suggests, it reflected the way that the ANC 'saw culture as an important weapon in the struggle against apartheid' and he emphasizes the generative connections that emerged during the festival as well as some of the organizational challenges it entailed. As Govan Mbeki, a leading member of the South African Communist Party and the ANC, argued in his address to the Sechaba Conference on 23 September 1990, 'Culture is a form of resistance to apartheid. But how we might transform facets of our cultural

9

life into weapons for the destruction of racism and tools for the creation and protection of the non-racial and democratic way of life we aim to establish is no easy labour'.[22] This discussion also sheds light on a neglected aspect of the European City of Culture year which has generally been seen as important only as a formative moment in the neoliberalization of Glasgow.[23] A sense of the broad participation in anti-apartheid activity was apparent in discussions at the *Banner Tales* workshop where many people recounted their experiences of helping organize Sechaba, hosting visiting South African activists and cultural figures, as well as attending the festival events and gigs.

To signal the banners' importance as material artefacts, Helen M Hughes, Textile Conservator at Glasgow Museums, has provided accompanying technical notes on the five banners that were the focus for these workshops. These look at the actual work of creating and using the banners. The banners reflect the materials, methods and ethos of the times they were made; all show evidence of the handiwork of the people who made them, such as the pencilled guidelines for lettering and hand stitching on pole loops. Most appear to have been made by artists or activists for particular events and were not designed to last, though four are now in public collections. The STUC Black Workers' Committee banner is different as it is still used as part of the Committee's activities. It is also clearly a professionally made banner, though from a handcrafted textile design tradition rather than that of a large-scale banner maker.

The materials and construction of each banner tell a story of their time and the care and creativity employed in their making; the use of synthetic fabrics and paints reflect the materials in common use when the banners were made; the kind of stitching and finishing are consistent with domestic or small-scale industrial sewing machines or equipment, and the pencil guidelines for images and lettering indicate the individual nature of each banner. The banners' condition – the signs of wear, creasing, paint loss and abrasion – reflects their use. These signs of wear are an important aspect of their history, and are part of the challenge for their future care, and the synthetic materials they are made of will pose other conservation challenges as they age.

The testimonies and banners drawn together here shed light on formative aspects of the experiences of the Scottish labour movement. They have significant relevance both for current debates in Scottish labour history and for the challenges of organizing in the current political context. These testimonies and banners also highlight the importance of recognizing and engaging with the diverse histories of the labour movement in Scotland. Internationalism continues to be a theme present on trade union banners in Glasgow. The current Unite Scotland/New UCATT Scotland banner, for example, includes the legend 'Free Palestine'. The stories here also suggest ongoing challenges which, arguably, labour histories can feed into. As Suki Sangha contends, in terms of the relation between BAME workers and trade unions 'We bring this wealth of experience into the trade unions and it's not always about conforming to the structures that exist but about adapting how trade unions do things, so we are opening up a space for more people'. In this respect, this publication seeks to build upon existing work on diverse histories of Scottish labour movements, to open up new conversations, and to signal the importance of material and symbolic political cultures. Raise Your Banners!

David Featherstone, University of Glasgow
Fiona Hayes, Glasgow Museums
Helen M Hughes, Glasgow Museums
Isobel McDonald, Glasgow Museums

Glasgow and the Anti-Apartheid Movement *Banner Tales* event, Glasgow Caledonian University Archive Centre, Glasgow.
Image © CSG CIC Glasgow Museums Collection.

[1] For example, Gorman, J. (1976) *Banner Bright: An Illustrated History of Trade Union Banners*, 2nd edn, Buckhurst Hill: Scorpion Publishing, pp.13–26; Nixon, M. (2018) 'Banners and Placard Poetry' thepeoplesvoice.glasgow.ac.uk/wp-content/uploads/2018/02/Nixon-Banner-.pdf (accessed February 2021); Pentland, G., Roberts, M. and Nixon, M. (2012) 'The Material Culture of Scottish Reform Politics, c.1820–c.1884', *Journal of Scottish Historical Studies*, 32:1, pp. 28-49; Stanley, J. (2013) 'With Cauliflowers, Kisses and Banners: 'community', radical politics, embodied activity and art in the early women's history network (UK)' *Women's History Review*, 22:4, pp.685–693.

[2] Crossan, J. and Featherstone, D.J. (eds) (2015) *Banner Tales of Glasgow*, Glasgow: Glasgow University; Crossan, J., Featherstone, D.J., Hayes, F., Hughes, H., Jamieson, C. and Leonard, R. (2016) 'Trade union banners and the construction of a working-class presence: notes from two labour disputes in 1980s' Glasgow and North Lanarkshire', *Area*, 48:3, pp.357–364.

[3] Griffin, P. (2018) 'Diverse Political Identities within a Working-Class Presence: Revisiting Red Clydeside', *Political Geography*, 65, pp.123–133.

[4] Peace March Scotland 1982, *Marcher's Booklet/Journal*, p.3.

[5] Jamison, BP (2003) 'Will they blow us a' tae hell? Strategies and Obstacles for the Disarmament Movement in Scotland' in Jamison, BP (ed.) *Scotland and the Cold War*, Dunfermline: Cualann Press Limited, pp.113–144; Eschle, C. (2018) 'Nuclear (in) security in the everyday: Peace campers as everyday security practitioners', *Security Dialogue*, 49:4, pp.289–305; McVicar, E. (2010) *The Eskimo Republic: Scots Political Song in Action, 1951–1999*, Linlithgow: Gallus Publishing.

[6] Gillespie, B. (2015) 'Springburn Young Socialists' in Crossan, J. and Featherstone, DJ (eds) *Banner Tales of Glasgow*, Glasgow: Glasgow University, pp.24–25.

[7] For more information about the exhibition, see https://www.glasgowlife.org.uk/museums/venues/scotland-street-school-museum/glaswegasians (accessed February 2021).

[8] We still have not been able to find information about this banner and would be very keen to hear from anyone who knows anything about it!

[9] For example, see Duffield, M. (1990) 'Black Radicalism and the Politics of De-industrialisation: the hidden history of Indian foundry workers', *Ethnic and Racial Studies*, 13:3, pp.442–444.

[10] 'Mr Balwant Rai Jain and Mrs Madhu Jain' in Raje, G. and Mahn, C. (eds) (2018) *Making Lives, Making Communities: Scottish Asians in Glasgow*, Surrey: Grosvenor

House Publishing, pp.22–25. The discussion of Balwant Rai Jain notes that 'The Transport Workers Union had a membership of Scots and migrants and the Knightswood depot's union shop steward was a Caribbean migrant himself'.

[11] On Black Sections see Virdee, S. (2014) *Racism, Class and the Racialised Outsider*, London: Palgrave, pp.155–161.

[12] See Kelliher, D. (2017) 'Constructing a Culture of Solidarity: London and the British Coalfields in the Long 1970s', *Antipode*, 49:1, pp.106–124; Anitha, S. and Pearson, R. (2018) *Striking Women: Struggles and Strategies of South Asian Women Workers from Grunwick to Gate Gourmet*, London: Lawrence and Wishart.

[13] Hirsch, S. (2018) *In the Shadow of Enoch Powell: Race, locality and resistance*, Manchester: Manchester University Press, pp.52, 60.

[14] Davidson, N. and Virdee, S. (2018) 'Introduction: Understanding Racism in Scotland' in Davidson, N., Linnpää, M., McBride, M. and Virdee, S. (eds) *No Problem Here: Understanding Racism in Scotland*, Edinburgh: Luath Press, pp.9–12, quote on p. 10.

[15] https://ucuscotland.wordpress.com/2018/11/12/22nd-stuc-black-workers-conference-report-dr-talat-ahmed/ (accessed February 2021).

[16] Cf Featherstone, DJ.(2012) *Solidarity: Hidden Histories and Geographies of Internationalism* London, Zed Books.

[17] https://www.gcu.ac.uk/archives/ (accessed February 2021).

[18] Massey, D. (2008) *World City*, Cambridge: Polity Press.

[19] Fevre, C. (2019) 'Scottish Exceptionalism? Trade Unions and the Anti-Apartheid Movement, 1976–1994', *Journal of Southern African Studies*, 45:3, pp.525–542.

[20] Raje, G. and Mahn, C. (eds) (2018) Making Lives, *Making Communities: Scottish Asians in Glasgow*, Surrey: Grosvenor House Publishing, p.53.

[21] Phillips, J. (2019) *Scottish Coal Miners in the Twentieth Century*, Edinburgh: Edinburgh University Press, p.179.

[22] Mbeki, G. (1991) 'Culture in Another South Africa' in Filling, B. and Stuart, S. (eds) *The End of a Regime? An Anthology: Scottish-South African Writing Against Apartheid*, Aberdeen: Aberdeen University Press, pp.216–223, quote on p. 217.

[23] Cf MacLeod, G. (2002) 'From Urban Entrepreneurialism to the "Revanchist City": On the Spatial Injustices of Glasgow's Renaissance', *Antipode*, 34:3, pp.602–624.

Peace March Scotland 1982:

Maggi Sale

The *Banner Tales* workshop at Glasgow Women's Library on 18 June 2016 was on the theme of women peace campaigners and marked the centenary of the founding of the Women's Peace Crusade in Glasgow, a movement initiated and run by women to bring World War I to an end. Maggi Sale, Convenor of the Peace March Scotland, spoke about the march that took place during July and August 1982, organized by the Scottish Convention for Peace and Disarmament, a broad-based umbrella group representing concerned opinion throughout Scotland. The march was a response to the Cold War nuclear arms race and its environmental impact, and its prime purpose was to 'inform and activate the people of Scotland in the cause of Peace'.[1] Maggi was chosen to organize much of the march and, despite her trepidation, being a single mother on benefits, took on the role fully.

In 2019 Maggi was interviewed about the significance of this banner (pp.16–17) as a symbol for the Peace March. She had previously used a dove symbol for her group HOPE (Human Order for Peace on Earth) in the Dumfries and Galloway area, and wanted something similar for the Peace March. Maggi discussed it with William Wolfe, former National Convener of the Scottish National Party (SNP), and while the march was not to be seen as a Nationalist march, it was thought that the banner should still represent Scotland. In designing the banner Maggi envisaged having just a dove on it; however, her daughter Gwen, aged 11 at the time, cut the dove into four pieces, with the saltire (the diagonal cross of the Scottish flag), and then separated them, which was then used on the banner. It was a deeply significant moment for Maggi: the seeming destruction of a precious object being born into something new was very symbolic.[2]

Over to Maggi...

'As I came in today I was just overwhelmed... I walked for a month. It took about a year to prepare for it and another year or so after that. So about three years of my life really were devoted to Peace March Scotland. It changed my life in many ways.

I had been in Africa for ten years. And there is nothing that gives you more perspective on your own society in particular than an absence of ten years. That was from 1966 to 1976. And when I came back the first thing that hit me was not just the materialism, but it was the blinkered ignorance. We took

Maggi Sale speaking at the Peace March Scotland 1982 rally.
Image © and courtesy of Maggi Sale.

Peace March Scotland 1982 banner
Glasgow Museums
PP.1983.4
2480mm high x 1380mm wide

Construction

This is a one-sided, single layer banner composed of one piece of fabric with the design painted in light blue–green and black acrylic-based paint on the front only. The fabric is a fine plain weave polyester with thread counts of 30/cm for weft and 36/cm for the warps. Grid and guidelines in pencil and a yellow pigment are visible on the front. There is a selvedge going down both sides, while the top and bottom edges are raw. The edges are covered in a 27mm-wide light blue tape which was also used to make six pole loops on the top edge. The tape and loops are attached with two rows of zigzag machine stitching. At the bottom a metal ring is hand-stitched to each corner.

Condition

There is some staining from the yellow pigment and ingrained soiling, especially by the bottom corners. While there are no holes or tears in the fabric there are losses to the paint and distortion of the metal rings. The distortion, soiling and paint losses are consistent with use, plus there is a lack of adhesion of the paint to the fabric where the paint goes over the yellow grid lines.

Maria Kontimpa carried out analysis of the materials of this banner as part of her MLitt in Technical Art History at the University of Glasgow, 2016–17.

PEACE MARCH SCOTLAND 1982

again that hit me was, well, the Chapelcross nuclear power station on the border [with England]. And they were planning to dump this nuclear waste in our local hills, our local hill Mullwharchar. So I had this banner in my window about the two signs of nuclear technology. It said it's not just the bombs, it's what makes the material that makes the bombs, and that the fossil age is over, or we are. What they were thinking of doing was this pepper pot thing where you cut a top of a mountain off, you put a whole lot of holes in, you dump the nuclear waste in there, put the mountain top back on, no one knows anything about it. And locals were all, exactly what's happening now with the fracking, "Oh but the jobs, and the infrastructure, and the prosperity", you know all this sort of thing. And I thought "Where are you coming from?" And I said "We have to save Mullwharchar".

"Oh is that somewhere in Africa?"

"No, it's your local Galloway hills that they are going to plan to do this in. Into the seismically stable hills that will never move, nuclear waste will be safe".

Maggi Sale's badge as Convener, Peace March Scotland 1982.
Image © and courtesy of Maggi Sale.

So that's what got me started in the whole anti-nuclear thing. As a result of that I was invited up to the (S) TUC Congress and eventually became involved in this [the Peace March]. And I'm telling you this personal stuff because... it would be good to get a lot of the personal consequences... it ended my marriage. And my husband was 100% politically behind this issue, but not his wife disappearing into smelly campsites and not having the dinner on the table and this sort of thing, you know. So that whole transition of women starting to open up to who we were and their men intellectually agreeing to it. So, it was a hell of a challenge to women at this time.

The Peace March Scotland was actually inspired by a women's march from Copenhagen to Paris the previous year [organized by the Norwegian Women for Peace]. And a group of Scots that went there including Billy Wolfe, the lovely Billy Wolfe, came back with the idea to have one in Scotland. Now the whole plan was to connect what was happening, again because of ignorance, a lot's happening in your back yard – "Do you know there is a nuclear bunker there, do you know this?"

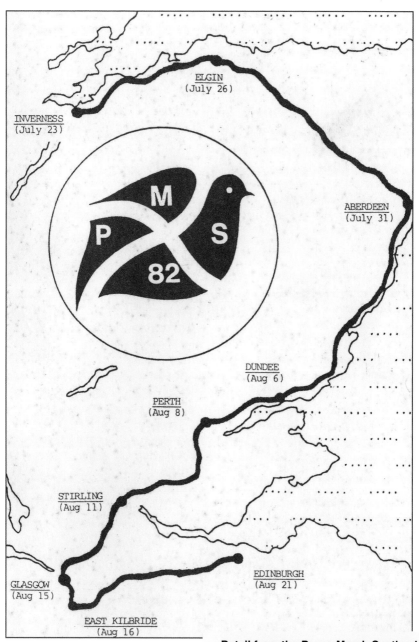

INVERNESS
(July 23)

ELGIN
(July 26)

ABERDEEN
(July 31)

DUNDEE
(Aug 6)

PERTH
(Aug 8)

STIRLING
(Aug 11)

GLASGOW
(Aug 15)

EDINBURGH
(Aug 21)

EAST KILBRIDE
(Aug 16)

Detail from the Peace March Scotland 1982 Marcher's Booklet/Journal front cover.
Image © and courtesy of Maggi Sale.

**Buddhist monks leading the Peace March
Scotland 1982, Edinburgh.**
Image © and courtesy of Maggi Sale.

So we decided to do this big number two (march). [It] started in Inverness, Aberdeen. I used to dream about this map, all the way down, Dundee, Stirling, across to Glasgow, then back to Edinburgh, lasting 33 days. And the whole idea in the preparation year was to get church groups, and union groups, and young unemployed groups, and women's groups working together. Again, this is a people's thing, it's people that have to make peace for themselves, for their family and community. It has to be based on knowledge, and ignorance was what was being allowed to drive this.

Increasingly it was women who were daring to stand up and daring to take the consequences, very often the personal consequences of a family breakdown, to do this. As well as working with the Greenham Common [Women's Peace Camp] group, a group of Buddhist monks came to lead the march. There was also a lovely bunch of lads, about 40 of them all together, doing the whole walk – they wanted to be out there in front with the militant slogans and things, and I had to say "Look, I appreciate what you are saying, but get to the back of the bus. Walking into a village you don't want to alienate people already, you know. You want to intrigue, attract people."

So we had the Buddhists in front all the way down. They came up from Milton Keynes and they led the march and just gave that cohesion of "Come on, it's peace". You know it has to be a peaceful approach to people, not something that alienates them or gives them the excuse of, "Oh that's nothing to do with me". And it worked, by the time we got to Edinburgh there was 4,000 plus.

So the march was momentous in my own life but the consequences of that throughout were communities of people coming together. Especially the young lads that joined, I mean they were a bunch of disaffected youths with nothing better to do with their time, you know. And by the time they got to the end, the relationships they were making with each other. Above all, the relationships they were making with the police, especially in some of the bigger regions, you had the same policemen on duty for three or four days. And by the time they got to the end, you know, really, communication was happening. And a lot of those bobbies [policemen] gave up their time to come to the rally at the end, and came with their families, and to me that was what it was about.

So if there was anything happening in the Peace March from my point of view it was how we connect. How do we connect individually, and as groups? Above all, how do we connect with our own inner core of what it is to be human? And until we have done that the game's a bogey [it's all over] because they are always talking about the differences.

There's a photograph of my mother leading the Peace March up the mound in Edinburgh. And she appeared in Stirling when the march was halfway down the country, basically to rescue my daughter Gwen who was also on the Peace March. She was watching it on the television, news reports, what have you. "And she's [Gwen] wearing the same clothes she's had for four days, you know!" So she came up to Stirling to rescue her granddaughter. Well, the granddaughter had different ideas and took her to a charity shop, got her a pair of boots! My mother walked for the next 13 days! She was very against what I was doing.

So I'd like to just read a wee bit from my own book *Dying Embers and Shooting Stars*.[3] It'll catch a wee bit of the flavour of the march and pay homage especially to Gwen. [Gwen was tragically knocked down and killed at the age of 31.] It's called 'Nellie's Call Will Be Answered'. [Maggi refers to herself as Margo, and Nellie is a pet name for Gwen.]

"Vivid memories came to her mind of her 11-year-old daughter walking along the roads of rural Perthshire at the head of a Peace March in 1982. We had joined all the Scottish towns from north to south and lasted 33 days. Nellie had joined it reluctantly a week after we set off from Inverness to enable her Convenor mother to carry out her peace campaigning and parental responsibilities at the same time. Within days however she was in her element, the mascot to the march as she fiddled the weary walkers through their pain thresholds at the end of a 20-mile stretch. Some towns would meet the march with a lone piper and the cities would often meet it with a band. But by far the favourite sound of the 40-strong core that walked the entire way was the sound of Nellie's fiddle. Her repertoire grew as the Peace March continued. And when the walkers were in a local hostelry of an evening downing pints and bursting blisters Nellie would be sitting on the steps of the Peace Bus sending her mother to teeth-grinding distraction as she scratchily practised the following day's tunes over and over, and over again. She [Margo] had set up the Peace March through several towns earlier in the year, setting up venues and hospitality for the core group and working out logistics of supply, toilets, water stops, first aid, for a growing body of people starting with 40 and finishing with 4,000.

Nellie is our pet name for Gwen. Within a couple of days of joining the march Nellie had established herself in the march band and together with a 6 foot 6 inches Swede, a one-armed Scottish harmonica player, an Irishman who played the tin whistle and Margo herself who kept rhythm on the bodhrán. Each morning as the march left their overnight venue, locals, who either supported the cause or were just attracted by the music, would join in for the first few miles, but would gradually peel away as duty called or their knees gave way.

The Peace March walking through Edinburgh. Maggi's mother, Mary Charity, is on the right in the turquoise jacket.
Image © and courtesy of Maggi Sale.

The Peace March Scotland 1982 Bus.
Image © and courtesy of Maggi Sale.

The Peace March Scotland 1982 walking through the Scottish countryside.
Image © and courtesy of Maggi Sale.

Then silence would gradually descend as energies became focused on putting one foot in front of another with eyes only being raised in hopeful anticipation of the Peace Bus being parked up ahead with food, water, and plasters. It was in the silence that the miracles started to happen. The first time it occurred everyone except the troubadour, the one-armed harmonica player and Margo thought it was a fluke, and they all laughed. The second time it occurred, Margo and the troubadour exchanged knowing glances and waited for the penny to drop. The third time it occurred a hush spread from the epicentre occupied by Nellie, who had expressed the first audible clue. Fingers were raised to lips and heavy walking boots became ballet pumps that barely touched the tar. Then they knew that it was no fluke. Nellie's signals were recognized for what they were and the march waited expectantly for the anticipated response. The pace slowed to allow the walkers to change their attention from their feet and instead scan the surrounding fields or even the distant horizon. Even if the Peace Bus was dead ahead accompanied by a Mr Whippy [ice cream van] and peripatetic foot masseur, it was ignored. Their undivided attention was on Nellie's calls, each walker intently vying with the other to see what she already had. Firstly she would "prrft" through thick rubber lips inherited from her mother. Sometimes once or twice was enough to achieve the desired effect, but usually it had to be followed by a deep neigh which reverberated at the back of her throat. That usually did the trick, especially if she increased the volume.

Occasionally, however, against mounting tension throughout the entire march, what was required was a series of neighs that pierced the air. But without fail Nellie's call would be answered. A jubilant shout would go up from one of the marchers, the first to see the living, prancing embodiment of Nellie's echo as it kicked its heels and sped with flaying tail and mane towards the source of its becoming. The march would often come to a dead stop, much to the annoyance of the police escort with a schedule to keep. But even they couldn't disguise a fascination with Nellie's gift, try as they might. Margo has always known her daughter was more horse than human, and she delighted in others witnessing this magic phenomenon which no one could emulate, try as they might. Nellie sensed their presence long before she saw them. And when the horses answered her call and came to the fence or hedgerow they would eschew the attention of all others except hers. And the rolling hills and fields of Perthshire provided the best of backdrops for Nellie's communing with her equine cousins, as recorded by the countless cameras of peace campaigners from as far away as Chile and Japan."

'I said emphatically all the way through it that making peace is not all about marching or protesting. If we don't take what we learn about each other, and above all what we learn about ourselves, into our daily living, we are part of the problem and not part of the cure. We can't kid ourselves on that the protest in itself is what will fix it. We have to take that into our own lives, we have to make peace with ourselves. I'm still at peace with family, certainly with the community. Now I'm working with refugees and asylum seekers and we are creating gardens and we work together and we celebrate together, we share each other's festivals together. And I take them and their bairns down to my village, that's working for peace my way, you find your own way.

Four years ago I was nominated, sounds very fancy, "Scotland's senior indigenous grandmother". My title is "Grandmother of the Burning Hearth", and that's part of the 13 indigenous grandmothers throughout the world and they are affiliated with the Dalai Lama. And again he expressed that a lot of this lies in the hands of women, western women who can't pretend we don't know. We have got access to it all, how are we applying that? And in my role of "Grandmother of the Burning Hearth" it is my commitment to what we do today.

There was a hard core of 40 of them that walked. As I said at the beginning, they were very sort of militant, unemployed workers and what have you. And all the banners that went with that. So yes, your banners are welcome, at the back you know. In that four weeks that we were walking together, sleeping together, in church halls, we had the smell all the time. A lot of them would start to divulge their stories. A lot of communication was happening. Three of them I took home to my village home because they literally at the end of the Peace March were homeless. So I took them home, one is still like an adopted son of mine. One ended up in prison sadly, and another one ended up in teaching, and he had been told he was thick as two short planks and wouldn't do anything. He stayed with me for nearly two years and the other lad ended up marrying a local girl on a farm. But through the march several peace camps and groups were set up. There was one set up outside Elgin because a lot of the lads came from the north, started up there, probably around three quarters [of the lads] and some came from Edinburgh to join at the beginning. But a lot of the ones [lads] were from the north, from Skye and what have you. In fact Skye came with a very big contingent that walked from [there] and then joined up in Inverness. And a few of the lads from there carried on with us. Obviously they had the time to do it, walk for a month, they didn't have jobs. The one common thing was that they didn't have a job to go back to. And yes, we kept close contact, a lot of them then just joined the peace camps and became residents in the peace camps. And through the peace camp involvement a lot of education was going on. And a lot of information that they wouldn't have had otherwise. And very dedicated people that walked the whole way, again gave their life to be in the peace camp, guiding these youngsters. A lot of them would have become very angry, bitter, militant. And that's how they started off, but by the end of it, again what they knew about themselves was what they took from the Peace March. There were a lot of very creative things happening as a result of that, it was a privilege to be part of that process. And that wasn't envisaged, that's what happens when you are living together every day. You're walking for 33 days and you're sharing everything, food. And there was one other wee bit that I would like to share with you. I think it was in Hamilton. My job each day was to go ahead of the Peace March and make sure you know, if there was a police change, see who was on duty and this sort of thing. So I came off the Peace March and got into the bus, or got a lift to the bus. Waited there until the police came and joined [the march]. And two police cars came up and I said "I'm really sorry, I'll be with you in a minute". By this time we were running out of money, and having to go to the market and get some bread and things because a lot of the lads had no money, they were unemployed. And I'd go and get bread and cheese, bananas, what have you. And so I just ignored them, I did that every day, the police would come. So I came back, and as I came back I saw the panda car coming up again. And the police came out, two of them were carrying six carrier bags each with bridies and pies, and they fed the Peace March. I said "That's lovely, we have quite a few vegetarians, especially the Buddhist monks". And they went "Oh right", and they came back with apple pies and you know. And they weren't on duty that day, it was their own time. Maybe using the panda car, but with their own money they fed the Peace March.

And a lot of relationships were building up between these young "yobbos" as they were seen – even in the eyes of the police – and the police. And I know in the end that one of them [the police] when he went back to Inverness, he also took one of these lads in and put him through an education, and he saw if you don't go that way you're going that way. And he built up such a relationship in the four days that he was on [the march] and understood what had happened with his [the lad's] family and why he had been rejected. So wonderful wee miracles like that happen and it was magic.'

[1] Peace March Scotland 1982 Marcher's Booklet/Journal, p.3.
[2] Oral history interview with Dominic Allan, University of Strathclyde Oral History undergraduate module, March 2019.
[3] Sale, Maggi, 2013, *Dying Embers and Shooting Stars*, Balboa Press.

Collage of Maggi Sale asleep inside the Peach March Scotland 1982 bus; and a detail from the Peace March Scotland 1982 Marcher's Booklet/Journal back cover.
Images © and courtesy of Maggi Sale.
Metal badge, Faslane Womyn. Glasgow Museums collection TEMP.643.
Image © CSG CIC Glasgow Museums Collection.

South Asian Glaswegians and the Labour Movement

This section explores different ways in which Glaswegians of South Asian heritage have experienced and contributed to the labour movement. It draws on the 'South Asian Workers' *Banner Tales*' event which was held at Scotland Street School Museum on 17 March 2018. The speakers were Bob Chadha MBE and Suki Sangha.

The *GlaswegAsians* exhibition, which explored the history of the South Asian community in Glasgow, had opened the previous year at the Museum. The exhibition included a section on politics, and an Indian Workers' Union textile was prominently displayed. Very little was known about this textile, so we hoped that the event would help to provide information about the item as well as to explore the history of trade unionism and activism in Glasgow's South Asian communities.

The first speaker on the day was Bob Chadha MBE. Bob had been introduced to Glasgow Museums' staff by Gurdev Singh Pall in 2017, during work on the *GlaswegAsians* exhibition to which they both contributed. Their support for the *Banner Tales* event was just as generous – both men brought along personal photographs and documents on the day, and both agreed to be interviewed for this book. Bob's talk vividly summed up a lifetime's experience of activism in trade unions, the Labour Party, as a local councillor and throughout his working life. It also allowed his determination, firm political beliefs and humour to shine through. Gurdev's interview, recorded in 2019, emphasizes the importance of contributing to the welfare of the broader community, an ideal which inspired his father's generation to establish the Indian Workers' Association, and which motivated Gurdev himself to become a union representative.

Suki Sangha came to the event directly from a March Against Racism rally which had been held in Glasgow earlier in the day. Speaking against the backdrop of the STUC Black Workers' Committee banner, she discussed the wider historical context, experiences and contributions to trade unionism of workers of South Asian heritage in the UK. She also positioned the discussion in relation to the broader context of Black, Asian and Minority Ethnic (BAME) labour organizing.[4] Her analysis and personal reflections emphasized her belief in the value of trade unions, not just in the past, but as an active force now and in the future.

In Conversation: Mr Bob Chadha MBE and Isobel McDonald, Glasgow Museums

Could you tell me your name and some background information about yourself?

Well my name is actually Balwant Singh Chadha, but over the period I have been known as Bob Chadha. I was born in a small village in India in the Punjab province, in a family of Sikh faith. My father actually had emigrated to East Africa in his youth. He was one of six brothers, three sisters... my father's parents were also villagers. We had a large family. Three of the brothers, including my father, were recruited by the British government to work building railway lines in East Africa.

My father was a blacksmith, we had a workshop in our own village; one of the reasons my father was recruited along with his two brothers was because of their trade. So they settled in Nairobi in Kenya. When I joined my father in 1955, he was working in Kitali, which was around 300 miles away from Nairobi. After completing his British railways contract he worked at a firm which belonged to another Indian businessman – they supplied tools for Europeans farmers.

Anyway, after passing Matriculation [national school board exams] in India, I came to join my father. I was only 16 and a half years old. He felt that I should stay in Nairobi with my uncle because he was of the view that I needed to improve my English and learn the African way of life. Quite frankly, Matriculation was considered nothing. So arrangements were made for me to stay in Nairobi. After a few months of private English teaching I decided to join the Teachers Training College, but I did not finish the three-year course because my English did not come up to the standard required by the teaching profession.

So after completing one year at the Teachers Training College, I gave up and joined the Civil Service, as a clerk to the court in the Supreme Court of Kenya in Nairobi. I thought this was a good start, but there again all court proceedings were in English. However, I passed a few Civil Service examinations and also learned the local language, Swahili, and I was one of the interpreters, interpreting between Sikhs or Hindus or Indian people and the Court officials.

I was young when I came to Kenya, and met a young lady whom I married later on – I'll talk about that later.

Mr Bob Chadha MBE.
Image © CSG CIC Glasgow Museums Collection.

The Civil Service job encouraged me to apply to England to learn something more, like law or to take a degree, because I felt it wasn't enough being a clerk to the court. There was no prospect of promotion at that particular time, although once you get into the Civil Service you start undertaking Civil Service exams and you may get somewhere. Anyway, at that particular time, because of the Mau Mau movement[5] and Jomo Kenyatta's rise, there was unrest in the country, and most people were worried as the political climate was changing. Eventually Kenya got independence in 1963, and the Kenyan government was going to nationalize jobs. They called it an Africanization programme, and they were going to expel most of the foreign workforce, whether they were recruited from India, or Pakistan or wherever they came from, even Europeans.

At that time I was also considering joining the African movement, but I did not join because Civil Service employment regulations restricted you. But I kept an interest and attended African rallies; I also believed that Africans should get independence from the British.

And cutting the story short, I had met my future wife who was in her last year of studies. She was our next-door-neighbour and I arranged with her that I should go to England, for study, and she would come to join me when she was ready. She was doing nursing, she wanted to do midwifery, and applied to Helensburgh Hospital for a midwifery course and job.

I went to stay in Birmingham with my brother and uncle at that time. Birmingham I had a bit of a problem with, living at my uncle's house. Generally speaking Birmingham was considered openly racist. I wouldn't say the city, but there were some patches where racism was openly practised. Houses were not given to Black people, and so I had to live with my uncle for a short period. I lived there for four years.

Anyway, I also had a responsibility to my family I'd left in Nairobi, Kenya. The family consisted of my younger sister, mother, and blind older brother. Anyway, slowly and surely, they all came and settled in the UK.

Before I settled down in Glasgow from Birmingham, the story basically is that I went with my wife-to-be, whom I later married in Glasgow, after she'd completed her postgraduate midwifery course, to see Helensburgh (where she was going to undertake the course). When I first visited Helensburgh, it appeared like 'heaven' to me. I fell in love with the town and I said to myself, 'Well, I'm not going back to Birmingham'. I did not return to Birmingham. And then we decided to stay in Glasgow. At that time again, finding accommodation was not easy – the same racist attitude was present.

Advertisements would generally say, 'Only professional or nursing or medical staff can apply'. Naturally I used my wife being a nurse as a means to secure accommodation. A Polish woman met me and offered us a room and kitchen to rent. Obviously a room and kitchen was a good way of setting up a family. I came to Glasgow in 1966, got married to my wife in 1967, and we had our first child in 1968. It was during that period that my wife was working in Dunoon Hospital [on the Clyde coast], so she was out most of the time and staying there from time to time, and I was staying in Glasgow.

I started showing an interest in community affairs, first attending a Youth Club in the Sikh Temple. I said to the boys in the club, 'Well, I will become your leader, if you want, and I'll expand that Youth Club'. It was not in an ideal location, and moreover, I found out that the Sikh community leaders were getting fed up with children making noise all the time. They wanted us out, so we approached the local authority and they helped us and gave us a school, and then we began to develop the Youth Club. We started first in Willowbank School, a popular primary school in the west end of Glasgow, and later on in Woodside Secondary School. Both these schools had a concentration at that time of Asian children. So there were plenty of children, plenty of activities. The local authority gave us some staff and one thing led to another. And that's how our early life was. And then obviously we developed into a big club, a kind of community hub.

Children playing draughts at the United Youth Club.
Image © and courtesy of Bob Chadha.

What were you working as when you first came to Glasgow?

Well, at that particular time, interestingly, my own development was co-incidental. I worked originally with Crittall, a big steel factory in Birmingham. They used to make windows and doors, steel doors, heavy doors, supplying building construction materials. They had a branch in Glasgow and they offered me the same job I was doing in Birmingham.

Once we settled down a bit, I joined the Scottish Co-operative Society, in Morrison Street, Glasgow, with more pay and better opportunities. The Co-operative was a socialist society, the Co-operative was of my liking, and they saw a little spark in me and developed me, and made me a supervisor.

Now, funnily enough, during this time I was becoming popular, having been the first Black person elected as a branch secretary of a trade union called NALGO [National and Local Government Officers' Association], and appointed as the first Indian-born Justice of the Peace in Glasgow, Scotland. That was quite a success story but was as a result of the work I was doing in Youth Clubs. As I said, the reason the Youth Club idea came in was political, you see. Around about that time in 1968, Enoch Powell MP made his 'Rivers of Blood' speech. When he referred to Black people, he said if the Black population grows at its current rate, there will be a white backlash and there will be community riots and blood will run through the Thames river. It was quite emotional, quite a frightening speech.

Because of my political interest in Kenya, I was also getting irritated that things were getting nasty in Birmingham. During the time I was living in Birmingham with my uncle I got involved with the Indian Workers' Association (IWA). I went to their demonstrations and other activities. I was young but I was also ambitious. I wanted to settle down with a family. So which comes first? I mean, there were all sorts of pressures on me. I was trying to cope with them all, I managed somehow. I may not have become a national leader but I did something good and made noise here and there.

Many white people helped me, for instance in the Co-operative Society, where Lord Taylor, the Chairman, felt that I needed further education and sent me to Ruskin College, Oxford, for a six-month training course fully paid. On my return, Lord Taylor promoted me to become a supervisor of the department.

The Youth Club was developing, because we took it away from the Sikh temple to the city centre in Willowbank and expanded it to the extent that it became a Community Hub. Over 200 youngsters used to attend. We needed more staff, so demanded more staff. Also at that particular time I was helped to get more training in youth work. Things were happening. I passed my General Youth Work, Drama and Leadership courses.

There were kids in the Youth Club who showed an interest in doing drama. So, because I had done a drama course, I started teaching drama. We built up three youngsters who were very good at acting, one of them, a boy called Bashi [Subash, brother of Gurdev Singh Pall, see p. 57], became an actor in later years. The other one became a doctor, Dr Harpreet Kohli. They were stars at that time. They acted in one of the plays which I wrote, called *World Population Growth*. It became a hit story in Glasgow, and was televised by the BBC Asian Network so we started getting publicity.

The Youth Club was not a simply a Youth Club, there were a lot of other activities taking place, such as organizing outings and a children's version of the political TV programme *Question Time*. That's why it became a hub within Glasgow, run by Asian people, but there were a lot of white children

Children's *Question Time* **event.**
Image © and courtesy of Bob Chadha.

in that area so it became a multi-racial Youth Club. The boys and the girls themselves chose the name, it's called the United Youth Club. The *Glasgow Herald* wrote an editorial column which I still have a copy of. And that is why the Club's popularity grew along with me. I was growing up and politically maturing. I re-joined a political party, the Labour party. I had first joined in Birmingham, but became active in politics in Glasgow. I tried for a Council seat, but I'll talk about that later.

Could you tell the story about becoming a Justice of the Peace?

The Justice of the Peace appointment came because the Youth Club was gaining momentum and was popular. Peter McCann, who was disabled, was fighting [the seat of] Anderston in Glasgow, and I was living in that area, so I helped him to win the election. He visited the Club and saw its success, and he nominated me to become a Justice of the Peace. I was the second person of Asian origin, but the first Indian-born, Justice of the Peace in Scotland. Bashir Maan[6] was another Justice of the Peace. This gave me a lot of personal publicity, established me, helped me, to go and look for the bigger picture. I also continued Further Education courses, took evening classes, passed Social Work Training, took a Postgraduate and Master's Degree in Equality and Discrimination at Jordanhill College.

Could you tell us about joining the Labour party and how that was? Was it difficult?

The Labour Party when I was in the Smethwick area [West Midlands] lost to the nationalist Tory party at that time. Peter Griffiths, known for his racist views, defeated Gordon Walker MP, who was the Foreign Secretary under Mr Wilson's government. I joined the Labour Party basically to help Andrew Faulds, a very famous Shakespearean actor, who was fighting against Peter Griffiths for the Smethwick seat. Andrew defeated Peter Griffiths in the 1966 election, good result. I played my part when I moved to Scotland. My wife at that time was busy in her nursing career and when I re-joined the party again in 1966 I started looking for a political branch. I became a member of the Kelvingrove constituency, where Labour was quite a progressive party at that time, with a lot of political problems; however, there were many strong and popular Labour people in the constituency then.

Malcolm Green, obviously, you know he was there, people like Kay Carmichael[7] who was a social worker, and Janey Buchan[8] and her husband Norman.[9] Some of them did help me later on, later in my life. In fact, there is a photograph of Kay Carmichael with me when she attended and participated in our *Question Time* programme organized by children at the Youth Club. It was the same as the Sir Robin Day TV show. We were copying everything British people were doing on popular TV or popular programmes. But they were popular and they were good initiatives, and appreciated by the children and general public.

Did you find there was any racism when you joined the Labour Party?

Joining the Labour party, there was no racism. But after that, you experienced it when you went to fight for a seat or a position. When I came to Glasgow I had a lot of struggles to find a seat. I did manage to find a seat with the help of some white members in the Whiteinch area, in the north of Glasgow, where I lived at that time, in a street called Morar Drive in the Partick area. It was there that I met Donald Dewar, a Glaswegian Labour politician who became the inaugural First Minister of Scotland. He was chair of the Kelvingrove Constituency Labour Party and he came to meet me at the house to recruit me.

Geoff Shaw, a Church of Scotland minister, used to be one of the Labour party leaders. I had met him through the Youth Club. He was from the Iona Community,[10] also a small group, with a big office in Clyde Street. (It was there, actually, funnily enough, that I met Douglas Alexander, father of [politician] Wendy Alexander and a Church of Scotland minister, who also helped me to organize a public meeting with a number of speakers from our Youth Club and the Asian communities.)

I fought the Whiteinch Ward in the Glasgow City Council elections in 1972. This was a seat which was not in a Labour area and which was considered to be unwinnable. But I still made some impact. The Youth Club at that time was still running, and it was its popularity which was getting me further and further known in social and political circles.

Could you tell us more about your trade union activities?

The trade union was another aspect of my life. It started, as I said, with the Co-operative movement, and we were all members of the APEX Union. I became involved as I was a shop steward, and the trade union became another part of my political activities. The six months I had spent at Ruskin College, Oxford, proved useful, as I became more aware of political issues. I was looking for some sort of position, power, where I wanted to be able to change things, basically, and being elected as shop steward in the Co-operative at Morrison Street helped me to link with the trade unions' side of politics.

At the same time Maggie Chetty, a Communist anti-apartheid activist and teacher, was one of the Community Relations Officers in Glasgow. She wanted to develop a link with the Asian community. She came to me and Dr Singh of the IWA. She wanted to start a group to encourage Black and Asian people to join unions at their work places, and she set up a group called SILC (Scottish Immigrant Labour Council). I became treasurer of that group. So now you are moving into the white establishment. That gave me more encouragement of getting further and further.

Could you tell us about when you set up a group?

The first group which I set up was in the trade unions movement. When I was asked by the Strathclyde Branch of APEX to set up a Black staff group who were working in Strathclyde Local Government, I was one of the few Black shop stewards within the Region. I was nominated to go to attend a conference in London organized by the national union, which a lot of other Black and Asian people were asked to attend. It was there the demand to establish at branch level a Black Section or Black and Asian Employee group was agreed. The union thought that if Black or non-white employee group members wanted to get funds from the union for training, then it had to be a national political group with a properly constituted framework, a kind of political group, with local branch groups as well. So I, along with another friend, Naryan Sood from Edinburgh, were the delegates and reported back to the branch. The idea was for us to develop the group through those members who were working in local government in Scotland, although remember local government at that time also included people working in health centres, police officers; mostly they were NALGO or Unison members. Anyway, we collected names of people who were non-European. You know, at that time in my social work activities I was already working on it. I knew how many Black people were there. So we gathered the information from all over Scotland, and first of all, set up a Black group within the branch. I was a key activist. Then seven or eight of us, there were more, who we knew could come not regularly, but would attend the meeting. We drafted a constitution, developed the group, trained the group, and went to several union training sessions.

UNISON trade union metal and enamel badge.
Glasgow Museums collection PP.2015.64.100.
Given to Glasgow Museums by the family of Andy Thomson, 2015.
Image © CSG CIC Glasgow Museums Collection.

It is interesting, at that time I had a family of three children. They used to come with me to union meetings – there was no crèche facility in any union at that time, but we created it. We, the Black section, helped to establish it as other relevant groups emerged. For example, Women and Gay and Lesbian groups, they all started demanding one. Now a crèche facility is provided in every union, every political party, even at some workplaces. Those are some contributions we made.Our political philosophy was a grouping of people getting together, thinking the same way, because they were generally suffering from racism, or discrimination; I think discrimination is the right word. At that time local authorities started learning that they needed staff who could communicate with the minority communities. They needed to speak to the women who never used many services, such as healthcare services. So we at that time started demanding that you should have a Black person sitting in there in the selection panel as complaints were coming in, 'It's always the white people who are selecting people. And therefore who are they going to favour?'. When we insisted as a group and demanded it, so it happened. Social Work started it. I used to sit on the Social Work selection committee whenever there were Black candidates in all promoted posts.

We recruited a lot of Asian people into local government before I left the department in 2007. In 1988 I was elected National Chair of UNISON's National Black Members Co-ordinating Committee for a year.

What date was it that the group was set up?

Setting up separate groups within the unions started developing around the 1980s in Scotland. According to my own studies, when I did a Master's Degree on the subject of 'Discrimination and Equality', at Strathclyde University Jordanhill College in 1994, it is around that time that some of the groups which were obviously necessary developed. Now there are several other groups, such as doctors' groups and this group and that group. There is nothing wrong with change, and people have to change according to the social and political climate of the country. It is the involvement of people which is important.

However, my idea basically was to join the mainstream, but I was not getting anywhere. I tell you, in the Labour Party, generally speaking, the constituency makes the decisions. But my branch would not allow me to get into the constituency, they sent their own people to vote. Slowly then, I used to get nominated by my union, the union started sending me constituency membership. I saw there were other groups to join, socialist health, I became their member as well, because you were not going to get nominated by the branch so you might as well get it from another section. Of course, later on I became a branch chair, even participated at constituency level.

As time passed, after several struggles and hard work with the communities, I was elected to North Lanarkshire Council from 1995 to 2017. The Labour Party also set up a Black section at national level, and I was elected Co-Chair of the Scottish Labour Party, Black Section Working Party, a position I held till it folded in 2010. That's what happened because we started doing it and making it happen.

It sounds like sometimes you had to find different approaches to get to where you wanted to be?

Well you see, this is what politics is. It's bringing change, bringing about change in the system. That's where the present leader (Jeremy Corbyn, Labour Party leader 2015–2020) was having difficulty with Tony Blair or others, you see. Tony Blair wanted to stay on as it was, nothing changed. He wanted to move on the right wing of the party, whereas Jeremy Corbyn opposed the war [in Iraq], opposed everything the Blair Government was doing or stood for. Most of us who were working in the Labour Party wanted more radical changes. You need to have the kind of people who can stand up and be counted and not become an established elite. Most political parties suck you in. They make you think the way the National Committee is thinking on a national level. It's the same even at constituency level, they will stop you at the branch level you see.

I remember when you were talking [at a *Banner Tales* event], you said something about 'you have to keep on fighting for what you believe in'.

Yes, I think if you believe in something, then you keep going, never give up or give in. I am getting old now, I've not got that kind of enthusiasm, but when I was young it was hunger, it was desire, I want to be there, I want to see what is happening. So then that desire takes you further, further commits you, further engagement.

Throughout your political career, did you see a difference in fighting for political ambitions, socialism, Labour party values as opposed to fighting for rights for immigrants?

Once you get into, I said the words 'sucked into', the system, you start thinking of the bigger picture. You know people are the same really, feelings are the same all over the world. People have aspirations, they all want to better their lives, better their future, better their children's future. For me, you see what

I wanted, obviously I wanted to see my children did not suffer any discrimination in the future, which I did. I don't want my grandchildren to suffer any more – their mother is Scottish, and they have had some problems, but you know, some attitudes are changing, and my struggles and efforts still go on. As far as I am concerned, it's not finished. You've got to keep the ball rolling until people understand and respect each other. I came to this country because of love, because of my wife's sake. I said I will sacrifice the Civil Service job. This is what I did. Birmingham was not a place that she wanted to settle in. She had already applied to Helensburgh. I was glad, I am very happy to be in Scotland. It was good that we made a move from Birmingham to Glasgow and are now permanently settled here.

[4] 'Political blackness' is a term used to group together people of colour from different ethnic backgrounds, on the assumption that they face similar issues, particularly around discrimination and racism. Some people argue that the concept is a way to unite disparate groups, giving them a stronger voice and more political power. Others feel that this blanket term is inappropriate, as it ignores the unique cultural and political situation of each community. In addition, many are offended to be defined as a group simply on the basis of not being white.

[5] The Mau Mau movement was the main anti-colonial resistance movement in Kenya and was subject to extremely violent repression by the British colonial authorities.

[6] Bashir Maan, CBE (1926–2019) was the first South Asian Justice of the Peace in Glasgow, the first South Asian councillor in Glasgow, a Labour politician, and was a community leader within the Pakistani and Muslim community.

[7] Member of the Independent Labour Party, anti-nuclear activist, university lecturer in social work, and policy adviser to the Labour government in the 1960s and 70s.

[8] Labour councillor and later MEP for Glasgow, a supporter of gay rights and the anti-apartheid movement, and involved in the Scottish Arts Council, among others.

[9] Labour MP representing West Renfrewshire, then Paisley South.

[10] The Iona Community is a dispersed Christian ecumenical community which works for peace and social justice, rebuilding of community and the renewal of worship.

Indian Workers Union banner
Glasgow Museums
Temp.15385
880mm high x 1020mm wide

Construction

This is a one-sided, single layer banner composed of one piece of fabric with the legend painted in dark blue paint on the front only. The fabric is a fine plain weave orange-red cotton or polyester with thread counts of 20/cm for weft and 35/cm for the warps. Pencil guidelines for the painting are visible on the front of the banner. There is a selvedge along both top and bottom edges. The two ends are finished with a 45mm turnover secured with straight line machine stitching at the top and down the length of the turnover.

Condition

There are a few faint stains on the back, but no losses or damage or signs of wear.

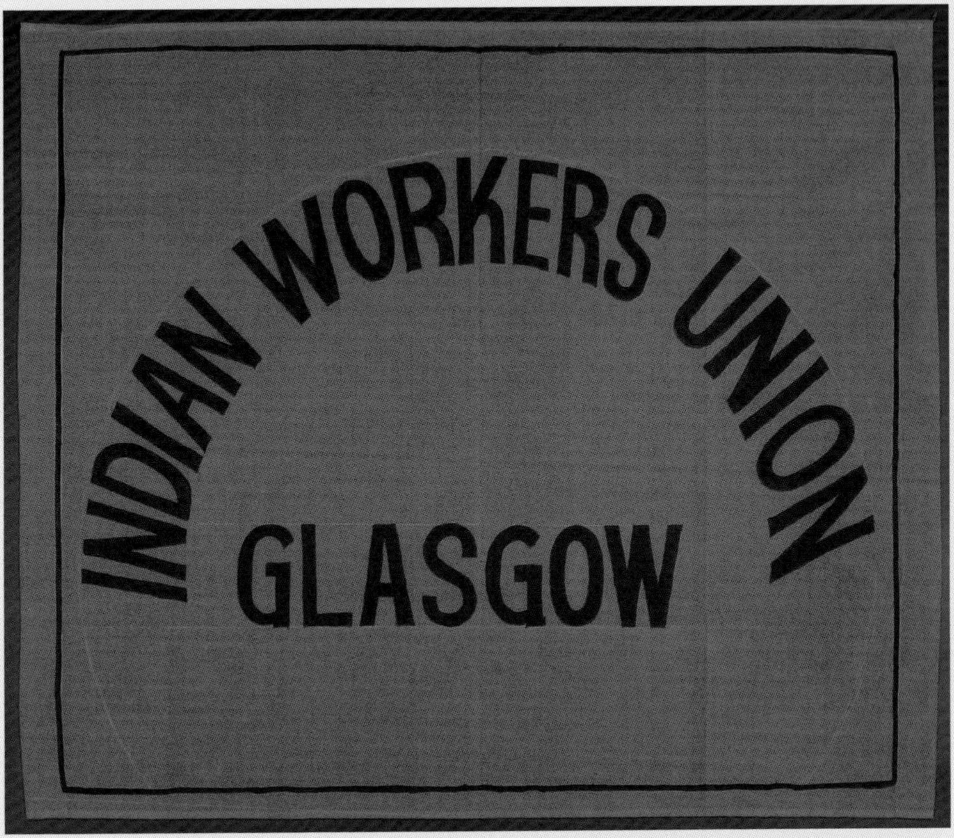
INDIAN WORKERS UNION
GLASGOW

In Conversation: Mr Gurdev Singh Pall and Isobel Mcdonald, Glasgow Museums

My name is Gurdev Singh Pall and I was born in Glasgow. We stayed in Logan Street in Oatlands, and that was in 1950. My family background is that my mum and dad came originally from India, a village called Galotian Kalan in the area of Daska in Punjab.

My father, Puran Singh Pall, was very much involved in community work. For example, supporting his father Jiwan Singh Pall, they both worked towards establishing the community as a kind of social structure. That would be through the place of worship for the Sikh community (the Gurdwara) and then following that, at some later period, my father himself got involved with the Indian Workers' Association (IWA).[11]

When the Indian Workers' Association started in England my father and his colleague went down south to attend these meetings, and after a short period of time spoke with members of the main branch and requested that they would like to establish a branch in Scotland. Permission was given for Glasgow to have their branch of the IWA in 1971.

Through being involved with the IWA, my father and members of the Glasgow branch raised concerns of the Indian community in the UK, but also a key activity at the branch was raising concerns about discrimination against the people of the Punjab. This is historically where the majority of immigrants who had moved to Glasgow are from. Punjab is a state in India.[12] So we're talking around about 1971, maybe earlier, when the IWA branch opened in Glasgow. The social environment was that they [the IWA] would invite dignitaries to the events, such as the Ambassador of India who represented India in the UK, and then similarly the High Commissioner in Glasgow who was eventually established there, and this was through the hard work of the IWA because everything was basically down south. Following on from that, they established a social network regarding entertainment, and showcased entertainers, dancers and play-back singers from the then Indian film industry (Filmfare India), who would come to Glasgow. Similarly we invited at that time, a gentleman by the name of Dara Singh (see p.52) who was the freestyle world [wrestling] champion. The hall where the event took place was Summertown Hall, Govan, Glasgow.

Each individual member hosted IWA meetings at their homes. I do recall my father having a meeting at our home – by that time, we had moved to McCulloch Street in Pollokshields [on the south side of Glasgow]. The membership at

Wrestling champion Dara Singh being met at Glasgow airport by Puran Singh Pall and others.
Image © and courtesy of the family of Ajit Kaur Pall and Puran Singh Pall.

that time of the IWA I would say was round about 18 to about 26. It was quite robust, probably more than that at some point. Later, the IWA became affiliated to the Labour Party as it reflected workers' rights. The community always, for some reason, voted Labour, so they had links with the Labour Party and through these [links] information was passed back and forward regarding events and such. And so representatives from the IWA would be present at rallies and workers' rights demos. Through the IWA movement, Indian immigrant workers were standing together supporting their fellow workers of the indigenous community. Throughout this period, there was the anti-apartheid movement against the situation in South Africa and Nelson Mandela being in prison. So again my father and colleagues had banners and such, and they were there on display representing and supporting the cause but also representing the IWA.

I started working with British Rail in 1979 as a leading railway man, worked my way through the system and finished working as a senior signaller. The union at the time I joined British Rail was the National Union of Railwaymen (NUR); later it joined with the Maritime and Transport Union, becoming the Rail, Maritime and Transport Workers Union (RMT) in 1990. Jimmy Knapp was the head and Bob Crow was his assistant. RMT meetings were held in the Glasgow Branch office, which was in Carlton Place.

National Union of Railwaymen trade union metal and enamel badge, Glasgow Museums collection PP.2015.64.634.
Given to Glasgow Museums by the family of Andy Thomson, 2015.
Image © CSG CIC Glasgow Museums Collection.

Trade Union march, 1980s, showing the SOGAT and SILC (Scottish Immigrant Labour Council) banners. Behind it, from left to right, are Puran Singh Pall, unknown, Baldev S Desi.
Image © and courtesy of the family of Ajit Kaur Pall and Puran Singh Pall.

I would attend meetings, not regularly in the early stages, but later on I was encouraged to attend, and these meetings were held in one of the rooms in Central Station. There was a trade union office, I can't recall exactly, somewhere in Glasgow and we did attend there also. And as time went on, I think the Labour Party decided that the Black and Asian community should have a voice, and they approached those who were part of that community in British Rail to form a kind of committee and be representative of that part of the Labour Party which was Black and Ethnic, as one would say. I was nominated by colleagues, and later on, was actually was the only representative from Glasgow for the RMT and would travel to London. Myself and my colleagues – my colleagues would be basically more so from the south, from Manchester, Birmingham, London area, Newcastle. Again they were from the ethnic community and we would obviously present our views regarding how British Rail should have us involved and also regarding the general political structure within the RMT, that our voices should also be heard regarding concerns and issues which were affecting Indian workers at their workplace.

Getting involved in the trade union, I didn't see any great difficulty. Probably at meetings you would be in a minority. And obviously, being born here, I was able to kind of mingle with, as one would say, the in-crowd, and from there a kind of rapport was established and it felt that, yeah, I could be supported in my views which I did give in general meetings with the RMT in Glasgow. As time progressed, I was eventually, as I said earlier, elected to represent the ethnic community by the RMT Glasgow Branch, and to attend meetings held at RMT head branch in London. The branch and the general union body decided that there should be a Black and Ethnic members group representing the community. These changes took place between 1989 and 1994.

The involvement regarding the community being Black and Ethnic within the union, I think we were quite against it in the beginning – you know, we are members, ethnicity shouldn't come into it. And it's kind of breaking up the actual ethos of the Labour Party but anyway somewhere down the line it came about that they decided 'Yeah, we should have this group of Labour supporters who are ethnic members from the Labour party, who are members of the trade union (RMT) to put forward their views'. So again, as I said, [members came] from Scotland and England, I can't recall anyone from Wales or Ireland from the ethnic community during these years.

Regarding the trade union, it obviously has evolved over the years, but equality in the workplace has lost its place somewhere. And that is that, as an employee you have a voice, but when you present it even at the meetings of the trade union and generally with your employer it tends to take a considerable length of time to have it resolved, if it can be resolved at all. So that's kind of what I would say about trade unions. Now again, yeah… obviously the RMT has evolved too. There's much going on just now, so hopefully they're more successful in the cycle of the various, as one would say, echelons. So, you've got the ground level, then you have the executives, then the further-on tier, and once they make their decision, to say 'Well yeah, we couldn't agree to that'. We are told through the media that the average worker is earning £500 a week, but I've still to meet the person that earns that kind of money.

Is there anything else that you would like to say?

No, I'm fine. I think it's basically around trade unions and the family's involvement. As I was saying, me and my six brothers and sisters are actually following in our grandfather Jiwain and father Puran's footsteps by being involved in the community and developing social structures which help the community, such as welfare and wellbeing and integration into the wider community. My eldest sister Sukwant, my sister Ashan and the youngest sister Trishna and myself and my younger brother Subash [see also Bob Chadha's section, p.41], we are involved in the community and have set up individual voluntary types of organizations, received funding and helped the community integrate, and attend various events such as we are speaking about today.

Can you remember anything apart from the anti-apartheid demonstrations; do you remember any specific IWA events that really stand out in your memory?

Not really. The one that does, as I said, was the rally for anti-apartheid. There was one other, which would have been in London, where the assembly was for the celebration of Indian independence and the injustice of what was happening in Punjab. That rally was also a protest against the Indian government, because the Sikh community in India were being unfairly treated. IWA membership was at least 300 in Glasgow. Up and down the UK the majority of IWA members were from Punjabi or Sikh backgrounds. One of the main issues was that we don't have independence in Punjab. There was that kind of struggle for justice.

Do you think the IWA was working with the community to hold it together? Was it the same people organizing outside the IWA as well? So was it the same people organizing political events but then also the community events?

Yes, this was very much the case, in the sense that every year elections were held. My father was elected as president, then later as secretary. As the years passed, he was elected the community liaison officer. These elections were structured and obviously constituted. The core of it was always the IWA members recruiting new members. It was robust in the beginning, but the core group of those involved and coming to meetings and such was about 26. The membership was quite extensive, maybe around 300, from what I can remember. They would come to IWA events and celebrate Independence Day and festivals. When it was a rally, the fear was that we were treading on toes because we were not part of the community, we could be pointed out and we would lose our jobs, so that kind of fear was there. Whereas my father and his colleagues were working in whatever field they were in, my dad was a shunter actually, in the early years, for British Rail, and his views and his colleagues' [views] were always, they were always at the forefront of these rallies.The community events, as I was saying earlier on, the festival shows and Independence Day in Glasgow were celebrated, and invitations sent out to all. Then a contribution would be given by the members you know, from their own pockets, and then obviously donations from the wider community. So, Independence Day/Festival shows were what were initiated in the UK by the IWA, these were the two main events from the movement that were celebrated.

Do you think that without the IWA the community would have less social cohesion?

Yes, they would have. The other organization that was about at that time was the Indian Association, and then we also had regular Sunday film shows coming from India, which we would know today as Bollywood. Again, it would be similar. The core group would be the IWA, so they would be part of the film association, part of the Indian organization because their mind frame of thinking was that these things need to be stabilized, need to be part of the community because the community needed to be aware, raise awareness.

What did you gain personally from being involved in the trade union? Did it help develop your confidence? Or your desire to get involved more in other issues?

What it did do for me was that it gave me the opportunity to be able to stand up and speak and give my thoughts. I would think of many things in small conversation, but... it helped me to be able to develop, to speak quite clearly and vocally of what were my views regarding whatever the situation was at the meeting. And a better understanding of how the trade union worked. So the various cycles of how you could be involved. Yeah, it did assist me... very much so in the sense of articulating it, to understanding the trade union and the layers and such. And then there were other things going on also within the trade union – as in life!

Are you glad you got involved with the union?

I enjoyed the time when I was there and again, as I said, meeting people up and down the country and then being able to become knowledgeable, as I said, of the trade union, later in life it did assist me. I was aware of various causes and such, these other things. So yes, in my employment, wherever I've had employment, I've always been kind of involved in... at present I'm part of a committee with Bield Housing Care who are my employers and it's to support the staff and develop ideas how we can communicate better and [how] facilities within employment can be a bit smoother.

Were you tempted to go into politics?

No. No. Regarding politics, I did join the Labour Party, I think round about 1985. I attended several meetings to have an understanding about the protocol of the branch. Later as time passed I realized that it was not what you know but who you know, pat on the back and drinking buds, you would get elected in the branch.

I would say that... I felt that my attention should be more towards my employment and my family, to allow my children to be more articulate in their life and move forward. My father similarly, always said 'Always earn your crust, don't be dependent on any[one]'. There was a social structure there that supported you if you couldn't work, but my father and myself throughout our working lives were not dependent. We've always worked.

So that makes the trade union a better fit with your life? It's about improving your working life?

Yes. Very much so.

[11] Jiwan Singh Pall and Puran Singh Pall were among the founder members of Glasgow's first Gurdwara, based in South Portland Street.

[12] These comments refer to the interest many migrants still had in their homelands. In this case, the reference is to the situation in the Indian state of Punjab and discrimination faced by the Sikh community there.

STUC Black Workers' Committee banner
Scottish Trades Union Congress
1440mm high (including pole loops) x 1860mm wide,
pole loops 110mm high x 105mm wide
Image © Scottish Trades Union Congress

Construction
The banner is one sided, multi-layer appliquéd and embroidered with the design on the front and a plain lining on the back, with a heavy tassel fringe along the bottom and loops for tensioning on each side. A synthetic 3:1 twill weave fabric on the front, thread counts approximately 70 and 130/cm, the lining a plain weave synthetic, with thread counts of 28/cm for warp and 34/cm for weft. The appliqué fabrics are synthetic, and a large central circle is made of white cotton. The appliqué has been worked separately then stitched in place on both sides of the outer blue/green ring. The letters 'STUC', the scroll and hand-sewn chain-stitched lettering across the top are directly stitched to the ground fabric. Straight line machine stitching is used for seams and zigzag for the appliqué and machine embroidery.

Condition
There are no holes, tears or losses. It has a slight dye run and dye transfer with separation of dyes on the white cotton from the red fabric or thread at the bottom of the white circle.

The STUC Black Workers' Committee Banner: Transcript of a talk by Suki Sangha

[This is the edited transcript of Suki's talk at the 'South Asian Workers' Banner Tales' event, March 2018]

I'll start with what got me involved in trade unions, what brought me into the movement and then maybe outline some of the challenges that Black workers face within the movement itself and often the lack of visibility of Black workers within the trade unions.

I joined a trade union when I was a student. My initial inroads into the trade unions wasn't because of the traditional industrial history of the workers' movement but rather the important role I saw them playing around social justice issues. More specifically, their visibility in the anti-war movement and anti-racist and anti-fascist struggles. While a student I got involved in the Stop the War Coalition, opposing Britain's illegal wars in Iraq and Afghanistan and campaigning against imperialism and the rise of Islamophobia. During this time, you would often see trade unions branches' banners represented on the demonstrations. You know, they were physically there. Certainly, in terms of some of the other campaigns I've been involved with too, whether it's around solidarity with Palestine, providing solidarity with people across the world, demonstrating to shut down Dungavel Detention Centre [an immigration detention facility in South Lanarkshire, Scotland] and making internationalism a core part of trade unionism today.

This was my primary interest in terms of my initial engagement with trade unions and my interest in getting involved in some of my trade union's formal structures and equality committees. I also of course recognized that when talking about challenging any form of oppression then for me that's fundamentally about dismantling power. It's about understanding and recognizing who holds power, and identifying that those who exploit us as workers often do so to enhance their own power. If you understand that capitalism – a drive for profit making – is what drives exploitation in our workplaces and creates the politics of divide and rule, then you also understand that workers as a grouping in society are incredibly powerful. Because as a group they have the ability to strike a blow to the profits of the ruling class by the withdrawal of their labour. It's vital that we understand how we build power as workers to challenge exploitation, to challenge racism and all forms of oppression.

So, it all connects together. And I suppose what was also important was the role that trade unions play in supporting anti-racist struggles but also families

Suki Sangha.
Image © and courtesy of Suki Sangha.

that face injustice, like the Surjit Singh Chhokar family, like the Sheku Bayoh family. Surjit was my uncle (my mum's brother) and he was murdered in 1998; the subsequent solidarity shown to my family and our campaign for justice will always be something that sticks with me. It's something my mum and grandparents often spoke about, visiting the FBU [Fire Brigades Union] offices in Glasgow, where they would often meet about the campaign and the trade union activists they met at the time. Trade unionists were there and kind of bringing solidarity in a practical way. So, that for me was quite important.

I suppose in terms of a Scottish context, I think the trade unions are active across civic society. Having a Scottish Parliament also means being closer to decision-making power which opens up space to campaign and affect change in a more effective way. Trade unions in Scotland can also play a much more vital role in fighting for the rights of refugees and asylum seekers, and can shape a much more positive and welcoming narrative than is perpetuated by Westminster. And, of course, we also have the St Andrew's Day March and Rally which is the only annual trade unions-organized anti-racism march that takes place across the UK and it is important that we march each year and put the arguments out and show strength in numbers and mobilize for that demonstration each year as well. Not in a tokenistic way, not in a way that makes the trade union movement look good because they've put something on, it's in the calendar each year, but actually to genuinely talk about how we can turn out and show strength on the streets and how we get more proactive in our anti-racism work.

I'm now going to address some of the criticisms that people have of trade unions, touch upon some of the history and also outline some of the challenges for Black and Minority Ethnic trade unionists who are active in trade unions. I agree with some of what has already come up in the previous conversations in terms of Black representation, representation of certain Asian communities, the Sikh community, that I don't see very often and also the racism that has existed within the trade unions historically and today. And for me, it's important that we do acknowledge and understand the fact that it was historically difficult for Black workers to get involved in trade unions. That there are numerous examples through trade union history where racism played out as a tool to divide the working class, and that trade unions often played a reactionary role within that. Also recognizing the experiences of Black and Minority Ethnic workers today and their everyday experiences in the workplace and relationships with their trade unions. Also recognizing that trade unions don't exist in a vacuum and of course racism is something we often need to address within our own movement.

Bob Chadha's contribution here speaks a lot about the fact that there was a need at the time to push for the self-organization of Black workers and trade union structures to reflect that. And that wasn't something that was initiated by senior white trade unionists. That was initiated by Black and Minority Ethnic trade unionists, and they were the ones that were actively involved in creating those structures and actually pushing down a lot of barriers that were put up. I suppose back then a lot of Black organizations seemed a threat, something the trade unions movement couldn't control, that they were going to shut that down in any way possible, and that's reflected in some of the stories that you hear from over the years.

It is true that any historical narrative of trade unions does also need to acknowledge the role racism played in creating division amongst working class people. Trade unions weren't always a welcoming place for Black and Minority Ethnic people. Migrants coming to the UK were often seen as a threat to white British workers, they were seen to be undercutting wages or were seen as a threat to British jobs. Those arguments were very similar to the arguments we've seen over the years. I think it's really important as trade unionists we challenge those arguments at every turn because those still exist in the trade union movement. The workers' movement is made up of ordinary people. We know we are all subjected to, and exposed to, reactionary elements of the mainstream press and we also hear the racist rhetoric of politicians. We can't shield trade unions members from that. We can however, challenge racism – call it out, show solidarity to those who need it, challenge and confront it, build unity and fundamentally our own power as a class. This isn't easy work but it's necessary.

It's also important to note that Black and Minority Ethnic workers know how to organize. Our history is rich in organizing in our communities, whether it be the civil rights movements, anti-apartheid campaigns or other forms of working with your wider community. We bring this wealth of experience into the trade unions and it's not always about conforming to the structures that exist but about adapting how trade unions do things, so we are opening up a space for more people. We also need to understand the types of employment that our communities are in. When no one would employ us, we opened up our own businesses. Many Black and Minority Ethnic communities are self-employed, they're not in those big, industrial sectors that trade unions are historically organized in. Many are also in low-paid precarious work. This means our organizing approach needs to recognize and adapt to that where necessary.

So how do we build trade union organizations for the future? It's going to be dependent on how we organize workers today, and work today. We need to make trade unions relevant to those people in low-paid and precarious work, build beyond just the traditional industries and win over migrant workers who are often subjected to the worst forms of exploitation. Trade unions will not be relevant unless we make the arguments around how exploitation works, how our labour as workers is exploited in order to make profit for the bosses. Where do we as workers get our power? How do we band together and build powerful trade unions? Why is this in our interests? No one will do that work for us.

We don't always hear many stories about Black and Minority Ethnic workers organizing in the trade unions. One story which is celebrated is the Grunwick Strike of 1976–1978 [at the Grunwick Film Processing Laboratories in Willesden, London]. This strike involved predominantly female, East Asian African workers [South Asians who had to leave Uganda and Kenya] who were fighting for trade union recognition. Their story is important because it challenged people's mindset and broke boundaries. Asian women were sometimes seen as passive, not keen on being involved in trade unions, perhaps not interested. But their story at Grunwick challenged those sexist notions.

There's a really good play going around just now. I don't know if you've seen it, it's *We are the Lions Mr Manager*.[13] It's absolutely brilliant, people should go along and see that. There's one scene which is particularly good where one of the workers, Jayaben Desai – one of the key organizers of the strike – addresses the manager of the film processing factory and she says:

'What you are running is not a factory, it is a zoo. But in a zoo, there are many types of animals. Some are monkeys who dance on your fingertips. Others are lions who can bite your head off. We are the lions, Mr Manager.'[11]

It's just a great example of understanding the power dynamic in a workplace and how workers fundamentally hold power when organized. The strike also managed to shift huge sections of the trade union movement who mobilized in support of their action.

Now to say a little about the STUC Black Workers' banner. I didn't actually know much about its history until I was asked to do this event today. It was produced by Ken Patterson and designed in collaboration with the committee at the time, in 2010 and 2011. The committee chose the words that are on the ribbon at the top, so, 'equality, unity, community, diversity, justice and freedom'. Really important words, reflecting our movement as Black workers. The colour green was chosen because it features a lot in African flags and people felt that was quite important. And the black and white doves are seen as peace symbols.

In terms of where it's been, it's been on lots of demonstrations over the years, whether that be to do with industrial disputes, social justice-related mobilizations such as anti-racism demonstrations, anti-nuclear peace protests, anti-war demonstrations. I know it's been on demonstrations confronting the far right. A whole range of solidarity protests across the country.

I suppose I also want to touch on the power aspect that I spoke about earlier, just to complete the session. The discussion about 'How do you get people involved in politics, why are there not more MPs, MSPs, councillors for the Sikh community?' For me it also comes down to what does power look like and how do we build bottom-up power? On the one hand we believe that power lies in the parliamentarians, politicians, or it might be we believe that power lies somewhere else, it lies with the vast majority of people; it lies within the communities; it lies in people power. I personally believe that parliamentary politics has some role to play, but fundamentally power comes from our ability as a class to organize and take to the streets when needed. It's when ordinary people band together that we get any kind of change. Equality, better wages, fair and decent employment isn't just handed to us. We have to fight for it.

So, for me, power isn't always about who we as Black and Ethnic Minority people can have as representation in the cohort of politicians, but it's about how can we actually build power from below. Far too often you get career politicians who climb the ladder and then drop the rope behind them. We want leaders who are rooted in our class and understand the struggle.

---

[13] This play written by Neil Gore toured in 2017. For more information, see: http://www.townsendproductions.org.uk/shows/we-are-the-lions-mr-manager (accessed February 2021).

Metal and plastic Anti-Apartheid badge, 1970s–80s. Glasgow Museums Collection TEMP.1195.
Image © CSG CIC Glasgow Museums

Glasgow and the Anti-Apartheid Movement

The final section of this publication explores the relations between Glasgow, the broader labour movement, and the long struggle against apartheid. It draws on the most recent *Banner Tales* event (13 October 2018), held in association with Glasgow Caledonian University which holds the archives of the Scottish Committee of the Anti-Apartheid Movement, and linked to a Nelson Mandela Scottish Memorial Foundation display at Kelvin Hall. The discussion was oriented around two key banners: the evocative banner 'Nelson Mandela – Freeman of Glasgow – Prisoner of Apartheid', which was created in 1981 by Jim Cathcart to mark the Freedom of the City being awarded to Mandela; and the banner of the Sechaba International Festival. The Sechaba festival and conference was held in Glasgow in 1990 and used the fact that Glasgow was then the European City of Culture to raise a set of questions about different forms of cultural resistance to apartheid.

The speakers at the event, whose accounts are reproduced here, were Suganya Chetty, who was a key representative of the African National Congress (ANC) in Scotland, and Brian Filling and John Nelson who were Chair and Secretary of the Scottish Committee of the Anti-Apartheid Movement respectively. Their accounts give a strong sense of the relationship between Glasgow, the labour movement and anti-apartheid movement, of the relations between, and the importance of, the cultural politics of anti-apartheid, as well as some of the broader dynamics of the movement in Scotland. They also give a sense of the different forms of labour and organizing that went into building and maintaining such a long-standing campaign – an important theme in the discussion at the event. In response to a question about how the forms of activism they were involved in then were different from today, one of the participants talked about the disadvantages of having to do huge amounts of mundane labour such as cutting stencils and writing envelopes for members.

Although the anti-apartheid struggle was successful, organizing work related to these campaigns continues. Both Brian Filling and John Nelson are central figures in the Nelson Mandela Scottish Memorial Foundation, which campaigns to raise funds for a statue of Nelson Mandela. The Foundation also does educational work which centres on both the 'life and legacy of Nelson Mandela' and 'the role of Scotland and Glasgow in the worldwide campaign for his release and against apartheid'.

Sechaba Festival banner
Glasgow Museums
PP.2015.20.1
1140mm high x 3400mm wide

Construction

This is a one-sided, single layer banner, composed of one piece of fabric with the legend in green and black paint on the front only. The fabric is a fine plain weave yellow cotton or polyester with thread counts of 30/cm for weft and 45/cm for the warps. There is a selvedge along both top and bottom edges. The two ends are finished with a 40mm turnover secured with straight line machine stitching.

Condition

There is slight staining from paint transfer which would have occurred when paint was wet, but no losses, damage or signs of wear.

71

Sechaba Banner Tales: Transcript of a talk by Suganya Chetty, 13 October 2018

Dear comrades and friends, thank you for the opportunity to take part in this event.

Sotho is one of the 12 or so spoken languages in South Africa, together with English and Afrikaans. In this language 'Sechaba' means 'The Nation'. *Sechaba* was the official organ of the African National Congress (ANC). It was first printed in 1967 and ceased publication in 1990 when the ANC was unbanned.

My father, MP Naicker, was instructed to start an international base for *Sechaba* from London. This publication was essentially to inform the international community of the evil, racist apartheid regime which existed in South Africa. I have lived in the UK for some 50 years now and I am a British citizen. I address you today as a South African.

After I arrived in 1967 to join my family in exile in London, the very first visit we made was to the home of Canon John Collins and his lovely wife, Diana, at St Paul's Cathedral. They headed the International Defence and Aid Fund (IDAF), which channelled aid and financial support to the families of political prisoners and detainees in South Africa. This was done clandestinely and co-ordinated from London. My father also took me to the offices of the African National Congress and the Anti-Apartheid Movement, which were located in Central London, quite close to each other. Though small offices, there was always a hive of activity as people came and went.

Before continuing further, I wish to read a poem to you, to put the South African freedom struggle in perspective. This poem (see p.74) was written by Claude McKay (1889–1948) in 1919, and was used to honour the death of Basil February, a Coloured [a term in common South African usage] commander of the first batch of guerrilla fighters making their way into South Africa. This was in 1967 and it was called the Wankie Battle because it took place on the border of Zimbabwe and South Africa. Here they were confronted by the far superior South African army and although they never retreated and stood their ground, they were all shot.

In 1969, after a landmark ANC conference held in Morogoro, Tanzania, the decision was taken to open membership of the ANC to whoever chose to join, irrespective of race.

Suganya Chetty.
Image © CSG CIC Glasgow Museums Collection.

If We Must Die
Claude McKay (1889–1948)

If we must die, let it not be like hogs
Hunted and penned in an inglorious spot,
While round us bark the mad and hungry dogs,
Making their mock at our accursèd lot.

If we must die, O let us nobly die,
So that our precious blood may not be shed
In vain; then even the monsters we defy
Shall be constrained to honour us though dead!

O kinsmen! We must meet the common foe!
Though far outnumbered let us show us brave,
And for their thousand blows deal one death-blow!
What though before us lies the open grave?
Like men we'll face the murderous, cowardly pack,
Pressed to the wall, dying, but fighting back!

Comrade Oliver Tambo (whom we youngsters fondly called 'Uncle OR') was then the President of the ANC in exile, while Nelson Mandela and the others languished on Robben Island. He once said in a speech, I recall, and I quote:

'In our beleaguered country there are four pillars that will bring down the scourge of apartheid:

- One, the mass mobilization of the people inside the country;
- Two, the underground structures of the ANC;
- Three, the armed struggle as led by Umkhonto weSizwe [the armed wing of the ANC] and;
- Four, the solidarity of the International Community with our just cause.'

We moved to Edinburgh in 1974 and I sought out John Nelson who I was told was a longstanding activist of the Anti-Apartheid Movement. As there was no ANC office in Scotland I contacted him for advice and help, and we started a small Edinburgh Anti-Apartheid group, selling *Anti-Apartheid News*, picketing supermarkets and boycotting South African fruit and wine, also calling for a boycott of Barclay's Bank for its links with apartheid. We also campaigned to have no sporting links with South Africa. Speakers went out into the community to educate the public about the evils of that regime. We held bookstalls at miners' galas. We organized joint fundraising with the Medical Aid for Palestine group and Chile Solidarity Campaign. We forged close links with the National Union of Students, the Edinburgh and District Trades Council, and the Labour group in the City of Edinburgh Council.

One ugly incident occurred in February 1976. Peter Katjavivi, who was based in London and chief representative of SWAPO (South West Africa People's Organization), the Namibian counterpart of the ANC, and Polly Gaster of the CFMAG (Committee for Freedom in Mozambique, Angola and Guiné), the solidarity wing against Portuguese colonialism, were invited by the Scottish Committee of the Anti-Apartheid Movement on a speaking tour of Scotland. The Edinburgh Students' Union invited them to address them in the afternoon and in the evening to meet the Edinburgh Anti-Apartheid group at the Edinburgh College of Art.

The student meeting was disrupted by a group of right-wing thugs, and that evening, after the meeting at the art college finished, we approached our car and saw that it had been viciously vandalized. The bonnet had been ripped open with a crowbar and the windscreen wipers mangled. Obscene racist literature was daubed on all the windows. Pictures depicting black faces with the inscription read: 'You may like him for your neighbour but...'.

This was clearly the work of the National Front. I was pregnant at the time, expecting our second child, and when I phoned my husband to pick me up he rushed over straightaway. The police were summoned, and they put it down to vandalism. The car was towed away and written off.

Now, Polly Gaster phoned me the next morning from London to say that the incident was reported on the front page of *The Scotsman* newspaper with the photo of my damaged car and the registration number in full view, too. Heeding her warning, I concentrated on the arrival of my child but was much relieved that Peter Katjavivi and Polly were safe.

Anti-apartheid activity re-emerged after the June 16 Soweto uprising in 1976 and the horrific mowing down of students peacefully demonstrating against being taught in Afrikaans, the language of the oppressor. Following the Sharpeville massacre in 1960, this further inflamed feeling around the world against the racist regime. The Anti-Apartheid Movement called for a massive fundraising effort as hundreds of young people escaped and sought refuge in the neighbouring African countries to join the ranks of the ANC, either as combatants or to further their studies. So, we organized each year a ten-mile sponsored walk for Soweto, raising funds for the ANC school which was set up in Morogoro, Tanzania.

I'd like to stop here if I may. Before I do so, I would like to recall and read to you a manuscript that was brought to my attention some time ago now, *Solidarity without Borders*.[14]

'In 1975 the editor of Sechaba, *MP Naicker, in London was looking for a solution to a faster and more reliable means of transport of the* Sechaba *manuscripts from London to East Berlin. They used Royal Mail but, in those days, the postage between West and East was anything but fast and reliable. It was the time of the Cold War.*

Entrenched in Central Europe there were two hostile military pacts: NATO and the Warsaw Pact. Without being a member of NATO, South Africa's apartheid regime was, in many ways, part of the global strategy of the Western pact.

In 1974/75 the ANC together with the Anti-Apartheid movement in West Germany broke the news of the nuclear collaboration between Bonn and Pretoria. The exposure was substantiated with documents found and smuggled out of the South African Embassy in Bonn. This scientific/technical nuclear collaboration contributed immensely to the ability of the apartheid regime to eventually construct the bomb and the South African Defence

Force and paramilitary police force were well equipped with vehicles, electronics, weaponry from West German companies like Daimler Benz, Siemens, Thyssen-Krupp and others. The other German state, the German Democratic Republic (GDR), on the other hand, supported the ANC and their military wing, Umkhonto weSizwe.

So, the two German states stood in opposite trenches in this historic struggle against the last bastion of colonialism in southern Africa. However, people's solidarity with the struggle of the Black majority in South Africa knew no borders. Sechaba *was one example of many.*

To solve the above-mentioned challenge with the manuscripts, West Berlin was an ideal place. As part of the 'Western world', this half city was situated like an island in the midst of the GDR, that is, 'the East'. MP Naicker, at the time the chief of the ANC's International Department and editor of Sechaba, *and an ANC member who was based in East Berlin, contacted the Anti-Apartheid Movement branch in West Berlin. One of their members volunteered that the* Sechaba *manuscripts be sent by post to his home address and he would then courier the parcel to its final destination in East Berlin.*

This courier service worked smoothly for many years, though it had its hidden dangers. As became known later, the South African Bureau of State Security (BOSS) was quite active in Western Europe. Bomb attacks on the ANC office in London and the assassination of the ANC representative Dulcie September in Paris are just two horrific examples. One of their specialities was sending parcels prepared with explosives or containing poisoned T-shirts to Anti-Apartheid activists.'

I wish to dedicate this story to my children – my daughter Humsha, and her husband Martin. He is from a staunch Catholic Irish and Scottish background. And my son, Navin, and his wife, Anita, whose mother is Punjabi and her father comes from Calcutta. They had to leave India during the time of Partition and have settled in the west of Scotland. Both are staunch Hindus. And, most importantly for me, to my grandchildren, Ciaran Dhev and Asha-Kate who are both Scottish.

---

[14] Despite our best efforts, we have been unable to identify the source of this extract. For more about the role that the GDR played in supporting Sechaba, see Ilona Schleicher and Hans-Georg Schleicher (1997) *Die DDR im südlichen Afrika: Solidarität und Kalter Krieg/The GDR in Southern Africa: Solidarity and Cold War*, Hamburg: Institut für Afrika-Kunde, pp.55–74.

Nelson Mandela – Freeman of Glasgow – Prisoner of Apartheid banner
Created in 1981 by Jim Cathcart to mark the Freedom of the City being awarded to Mandela (then still imprisoned on Robben Island)
Glasgow Caledonian University
1240mm high (including pole loops) x 1660mm wide, pole loops 120mm wide x 120mm high
Image © Glasgow Caledonian University Archive Centre

Construction
This is a one-sided, single layer painted banner composed of one main piece of fabric and five pole loops of the same fabric. The fabric is a heavy-duty plain weave cotton canvas with thread counts of 14/cm and 18/cm. The design is predominantly in greys and black, with more vibrant colours used for impact. Raw edges on each side are turned to the back and held in place with a straight line machine stitch and covered with gummed brown paper. The front edges of the pole loops are attached with fold stitching, and the back with two points of hand stitching. A black coated yellow metal grommet is in each of the bottom corners.

Condition
There are no holes or tears in the fabric or major loss of paint. There is some abrasion and localized losses of paint, the outer pole loops are loose and much of the brown paper is missing.

Nelson Mandela and Brian Filling,
9 October 1993.
Image © and courtesy of Alan Wylie.

Sechaba International Conference and Festival: Cultural resistance to apartheid, Glasgow, 1990: Brian Filling

The Sechaba International Conference and Festival was held in Glasgow in 1990. Suganya talked about *Sechaba*, the African National Congress journal, the editor of which was her father, MP Naicker, one of the outstanding leaders of the African National Congress (ANC). The Indian community in South Africa was very active in the struggle against apartheid, including Gandhi, who was one of the key figures in the early movement. Suganya and many others ended up in exile.

In 1990 Glasgow was designated European City of Culture. We had some time to plan for this so we held discussions with the ANC and established a company, Sechaba Festivals Ltd., and set about raising money. The ANC saw culture as an important weapon in the struggle against apartheid, and we had hosted many ANC cultural groups prior to 1990, including Mayibuye and Amandla,[15] with great success. The title chosen for the event was the 'Sechaba International Conference and Festival: cultural resistance to apartheid'.

1990 was an important year for other reasons – Nelson Mandela was released on 11 February 1990.

The Sechaba Board was comprised of myself as Chair and John Nelson from the Scottish Commitee of the Anti-Apartheid Movement, and Campbell Christie and Pat Kelly from the Scottish Trades Union Congress. Frank Maguire, a lawyer, advised us on creating the company and other legal matters, and he attended Board meetings. Jim Tait was appointed full-time Director and we employed several others including Gordon McDougall and Noeleen O'Hara.

Programme for the International Conference of Cultural Resistance to Apartheid, Sechaba, Glasgow, 1990. Glasgow Museums collection PP.2015.20.2. Given to Glasgow Museums.
Image © CSG CIC Glasgow Museums

We also had a lot of volunteers who looked after different aspects of the festival and the conference. Our ambitious plans involved literally hundreds of people, not just as audiences, but many activists who were involved in the organization.

We worked closely with the ANC including Mendi Msimang, ANC Chief Representative in the UK; Mandla Langa, the novelist; and Mongane Wally Serote, the poet and ANC Cultural Attaché in the UK. There were quite a number of South African students in exile with whom we worked, in particular Lentswe Mokgatle, known as 'Eric' at the time, who was studying at Edinburgh University. Lentswe was very important in terms of the musical side of things. Volunteers did all kinds of things, organizing, accommodating incoming South Africans, producing materials, dealing with the media and so on. ANC recruited a group of young South Africans to perform. They came over from South Africa and became known as the 'Sechaba Group'. Prior to the Festival they performed around Scotland, including spending a week on Iona. They made a great impact.

The Conference and Festival opened on 23 September 1990. The opening session was held in the Banqueting Hall of the City Chambers, Glasgow, and the speakers included Pat Lally, Council Leader; Campbell Christie, General Secretary of the Scottish Trades Union Congress; and Archbishop Trevor Huddleston. I chaired the opening session, and in introducing the keynote speaker, Govan Mbeki, I explained why he was called Govan. He was named after the first Principal of Lovedale Institution [in Eastern Cape Province], William Govan, a Glasgow missionary. Govan Mbeki, one of the Rivonia Trialists along with Mandela, spent 25 years in prison, mainly on Robben Island.

Govan's speech was entitled 'Culture in the Struggle for a New South Africa', and it was subsequently published in the book *The End of a Regime? An Anthology of Scottish–South African Writing Against Apartheid*. He opened his speech by saying, 'I am particularly pleased and honoured to be in Glasgow as I consider myself an honorary Scotsman. Ever since I learned that I was named after William Govan of the Glasgow Missionary Society I have had a burning desire to visit the country of this wonderful human being and educationalist'. He also said in the context of culture and the struggle for a new South Africa that the ANC saw the 1976 Soweto Uprising as a key turning point in the struggle. The ANC had been decapitated by the Rivonia Trial, with its key leaders being imprisoned followed

Flyer for Sechaba's Mandela Club at 'Rain', upstairs at Nico's, 375 Sauchiehall Street, Glasgow. Glasgow Museums collection PP.2015.20.3. Given to Glasgow Museums.
Image © CSG CIC Glasgow Museums Collection.

MANDELA CLUB

at 'RAIN'
UPSTAIRS NICO'S
375 SAUCHIEHALL STREET

SOUNDS OF AFRICA

WORLD MUSIC

★ ★ MORE MANDELA CLUB NITES ★ ★

SEPTEMBER NITES

SAT. 1st • SAT. 8th • SAT. 15th • SAT. 22nd
SUN. 23rd • THUR. 27th • FRI. 28th • SAT. 29th
and SUN. 30th

OCTOBER NITES

THUR. 4th • FRI. 5th • SAT. 6th • SUN. 7th

10 PM   TILL   LATE

**Freedom of the City of Glasgow, 4 August 1981.
Left to right, Ruth Mompati, ANC, Brian Filling,
Chair of AAM, Alex Ekwueme, Vice-President of
Nigeria, and Glasgow's Lord Provost Michael Kelly.**
Image © Kevin Buchanan and courtesy of Brian Filling.

Sechaba Festival: Launch of a setting for choir, saxophone and orchestra of Wally Serote's poem 'I Will Wait' by Glasgow composer, now Professor, William Sweeney. This was commissioned by the Sechaba Festival of Cultural Resistance to Apartheid, and premiered in Glasgow City Halls, September 1990. Left to right: Tommy Smith, William Sweeney, Donald McIntosh, Jim Tait.

Image © and courtesy of Alan Wylie.

by a massive clampdown on the struggle. The Soweto Uprising by school students was against Afrikaans being imposed as the language for teaching. This uprising brought a new generation into the fight for liberation and many left the country to join the armed struggle.

The conference had many different sessions and involved key figures in the international solidarity movement, including general secretaries from all the leading trade unions in Britain.

The Festival included art, theatre, a comedy night, a writers' evening, a late-night Mandela club, and a lot of music. In terms of art, we ran an exhibition of the work of John Muafangejo, a Namibian artist, whose works now sell for a high price. Rev. John Riches of the Balmore Trust had a lot of these original pieces of artwork but they weren't framed. So, one of the contributions that Sechaba made was to pay for their framing, and the exhibition was held in the Theatre Royal, Glasgow.

I asked Abdul Minty to open the exhibition and he said, 'What do I know about art? I run the world campaign against military collaboration with South Africa'. I remember jokingly saying, 'Well, Abdul, this will maybe civilize you!' In fact, Abdul was very civilized and cultured but he was reluctant, saying, 'I'm just not seen as being involved in the cultural world'. Afterwards he said it was one of the best things he had done. I'm glad to say I became very close friends with Abdul. It was through him that I was sent as the representative of all the European Anti-Apartheid Movements to the United Nations Special Committee Against Apartheid in New York later that year for the meeting to discuss ending the cultural boycott. Abdul became the South African Ambassador to the United Nations in Geneva and he invited myself and Mary, my wife, to stay with him for a few days in 2013 and, of course, by this time it was quite different circumstances with South Africa no longer a pariah among nations, compared to when Abdul came to Glasgow in 1990.

During the Sechaba Festival we took South African plays and theatre groups out into the community, to Castlemilk, Easterhouse, Drumchapel and various other places round Glasgow. We set up a music sub-committee, which included Bruce Findlay, the manager of Simple Minds and a great supporter. Simple Minds was the first band to agree to perform at the inaugural Mandela Wembley concert in 1988. This was crucial in terms of getting other big acts on board because some of their agents were very reluctant, saying, 'It is not commercially very clever to be associated with this'. But, eventually, it got to the point where no leading artist could afford not to be part of the Wembley concert.

We ran a folk club in the Riverside Club for a week, organized by George Reid. Many of the top folk singers from Scotland and elsewhere participated, including Archie Fisher, Hamish Imlach, Rab Noakes, Michael Marra, Roy Bailey, the Humpff Family and Arthur Johnstone. It was very successful and busy every night.

We had commissioned Bill Sweeney, the Scottish composer, to write a piece of music for the Festival. His composition was based on a poem by Wally Serote called 'I Will Wait'. This was its first performance and it was given by the Scottish Chamber Orchestra, the Scottish Philharmonic singers, the Association of South African Students Choir, and Tommy Smith, the saxophonist, as soloist. When the concert finished, to a standing ovation, Bill Sweeney and Mongane Wally Serote joined the musicians on stage. All the South Africans began toyi-toyi-ing [a Southern African dance associated with protest and struggle] and soon the whole audience in the City Hall was dancing.

To conclude, there was an internal joke among our key people, coined, I think, by Chris Bartter, who was very involved in Sechaba, calling it 'Seshambles'! It was hand-to-mouth, we never knew if we would find the money for this and that to make things happen.

In retrospect, I have been thinking, 'How successful was Sechaba? Did it make much of an impact?' Laurie Flynn, who had worked for ITV's *World in Action*, and had made a number of films, attended the conference and saw the John Muafangejo exhibition. He decided to make a film about Muafangejo and his work, recruiting Noeleen O'Hara, one of the Sechaba Festival staff, to do the research. It was broadcast on ITV to much critical acclaim, so there was that very positive outcome.

The book, *The End of a Regime? An Anthology of Scottish-South African Writing Against Apartheid*, edited by myself and Susan Stuart, includes Govan Mbeki's keynote conference speech, 'Culture in the Struggle against Apartheid', poems by Mazisi Kunene and Mzwakhe Mbuli; Mongane Wally Serote's 'I Will Wait'; and pieces by Sol T. Plaatje, Olive Schreiner, Alex La Guma and Achmat Dangor, among other South Africans. The Scottish contributors included David Livingstone, Robert Louis Stevenson, Edwin Morgan, Naomi Mitchison, Hugh MacDiarmid, Jackie Kay, Jim Kelman and Alasdair Gray.

Lentswe Mokgatle introduced me to his friend, Marah Louw, the South African singer, on one occasion when I was visiting South Africa and we became close friends. I invited her to Glasgow and she sang and danced on stage in George Square with Nelson Mandela when he received the Freedoms of the nine UK cities. Following Mandela's visit we organized an ANC fund-raising tour for Marah and her band in the run-up to the first democratic elections in South Africa, in April 1994.

In the December following the election, we took a 33-strong Scottish delegation to the new South Africa, and Govan Mbeki, then Deputy President of the Senate, hosted the delegation in the South African Parliament in Cape Town. Govan's historical connection with Scotland and his contribution to Sechaba had cemented relations.

When I think about Sechaba, I no longer think about the difficulties, I think about the impact it had and the development and solidifying of relations between us and the new South Africa. The Sechaba International Conference and Festival was a huge success and worth all the effort.

Metal Anti-Apartheid badge, 1995, distributed amongst British trade unionists.
Glasgow Museums collection PP.2015.64.1138.
Given to Glasgow Museums by the family of
Andy Thomson, 2015.
Image © CSG CIC Glasgow Museums Collection.

[15] Mayibuye was the ANC cultural group, led by Barry Feinberg and James Phillips, the fine South African baritone, who visited Scotland in 1979. Amandla was the ANC Cultural Ensemble, led by Jonas Gwanga, the South African trombonist who was nominated for a Grammy award for the music in the film *Cry Freedom*. Amandla toured Scotland in 1985 and played to sell-out audiences, including one week at the Edinburgh Festival.

Glasgow and the Anti-Apartheid Movement up to 1981: John Nelson

The Freedom of the City from Glasgow to Nelson Mandela in 1981, and his visit 12 years later to receive it, didn't just arise out of the blue. The Anti-Apartheid Movement had been working for years to raise awareness of apartheid and the need to end collaboration with it, and local authorities had been an important part of that for a long time.

I only joined the Anti-Apartheid Movement in 1966, but I soon heard how six years earlier the Sharpeville massacre of 69 protestors had led to a worldwide wave of revulsion, to money and companies leaving South Africa in panic, and UN General Assembly sanctions. As part of that wave, Aberdeen Corporation [the City Council], had declared a boycott of all South African goods for any of its purchases. In the scheme of things, that might seem quite a minor gesture, but it caused a big reaction both here and also, I've been told, in South Africa. I heard some years later how the name of Aberdeen was still reviled in white South Africa. Among all the upheavals of 1960 this had hurt, especially among those with Scottish connections. Local authorities have an audience, a voice that carries a long way, which has been an important asset for us when they have taken action. I believe Bob Hughes had a lot to do with the Council's decision. He was a city councillor before he became an MP. He's now ACTSA's (Action for Southern Africa) Honorary President after a lifetime of service to the anti-apartheid cause.

In South Africa the Sharpeville massacre led to the African National Congress's (ANC) decision to launch the armed struggle, led by Nelson Mandela, and four years later he and much of the ANC leadership were jailed for life for sabotage.

I believe the Edinburgh and Glasgow groups started in about 1964, though I've never seen proof of that. Here they arose partly out of interest from those who had campaigned earlier against the Central African Federation [the union of the British colonies of Northern and Southern Rhodesia and Nyasaland, 1953–63] through SCAQ – the Scottish Council for African Questions. The Stop the 70 Tour campaign against the 1969 Springbok rugby tour and the planned but cancelled cricket tour raised the profile of the Movement, in addition to their more routine and persistent campaigning.

I only moved to Glasgow in 1972 so I can't really speak for the quite substantial work done here in the early days, and I never knew Cecil Williams. Cecil was a South African ANC activist, best known for being arrested in 1962 with

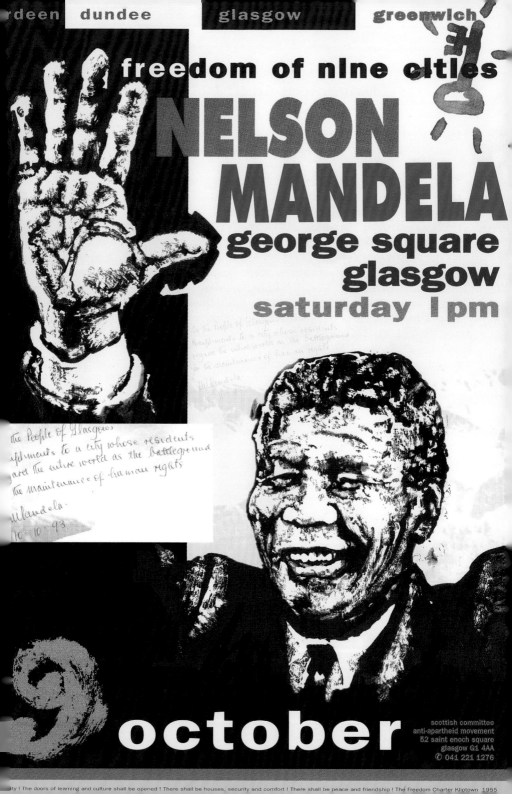

Mandela, who was posing as his chauffeur. A theatre director by profession, in exile he settled in Glasgow and played a key role in establishing the local Anti-Apartheid group there.

As Edinburgh Secretary I was in touch with Iain Whyte and Malcolm May about speaking tours and the like, including a tour by Bishop Colin Winter just after his expulsion from Namibia [for speaking out against apartheid], and I became Glasgow Secretary when I moved through.

In 1974 the new Scottish local authorities were elected – the two-tier District and Regional Councils. They had a year as shadow authorities before taking over, so we thought that was a good time to try to spread the boycott to the new councils as they were establishing their policies and ways of working.

The Glasgow Group covered the West of Scotland over to the West Lothian border, where the West Lothian Group began. The Glasgow Group therefore started writing to the new councils to ask them to boycott South African and Namibian goods. Councils were quite big economic players in their own right, and their decisions were also public and potentially very influential in creating awareness and a climate of opinion. The majority in Scotland were Labour controlled and so basically supportive of our aims. Glasgow District was very keen and agreed to the boycott. Strathclyde Region, the upper tier authority with a much bigger budget since it provided education and social work for half of Scotland, said they would delay a decision until they took control in 1975, but did then agree to it. Most of the Districts surrounding Glasgow also agreed. They were all quite small, mostly covering one or two small towns. I moved to Hamilton in 1974, and a local building contractor I knew told me that all tender documents for Hamilton District Council now specified that no South African or Namibian materials could be used.

It became a bit embarrassing to be writing as the Glasgow Group to Councils that didn't feel any connection with Glasgow, so in 1975 the Scottish Anti-Apartheid groups, which had been holding regular meetings to co-ordinate their activities, created the Scottish Committee to get over this problem and also to allow us to write more confidently to Scottish-level bodies like the STUC.

It was really just a letterhead, and myself as Secretary, and the meetings were the same informal co-ordinating meetings of local group representatives that we had been having. I've still got the little A/A symbol printing block we got made for the

Freedom of the Nine Cities Nelson Mandela poster, 1993, signed by Nelson Mandela 'To the People of Glasgow, Compliments to a city whose residents regard the entire world as the battleground for the maintenance of human rights, N Mandela 10.10.93', Glasgow Museums collection PP.2007.3.
Image © CSG CIC Glasgow Museums Collection.

letterhead, in those days of letterpress printing.

A year later it was agreed to establish the Scottish Committee as a more formal structure, with a constitution, a set of officers and a bank account, and the rest is history, as they say, or at least a bit better documented. A Local Groups Conference had been organized in Dundee for that day, with Abdul Minty speaking [Honorary Secretary of the British Anti-Apartheid Movement], so a business section was tacked on to deal with these formalities. It turned out to be three days after the Soweto shootings.

Political prisoners were one of AAM's campaign themes, and in 1977 there was quite a big international campaign for the Pretoria 12 and other political prisoners, with an international petition to the UN. We got postcards and leaflets for that as well as petitions, and held a torchlight procession in Glasgow the night before the petition was presented to the UN in New York on Human Rights Day (10 December) that year.

Work with local authorities went on as issues came up, especially about advice on sports contacts and meetings with South African officials. In 1978 we wrote to ask Councils not to meet with the Director of Education for Cape Province, and George Foulkes, Chair of Education in Lothian Region, asked if we could write a letter to his committee asking it to adopt a policy of not meeting South African official representatives, which would make decisions simpler in future. We wrote to all Regional Councils about this.

Against this background, in 1978 and 1979 Lord Provost of Glasgow David Hodge decided to give lunch to two successive South African ambassadors. The first of these caused outrage and provoked a demonstration of 1,000 people in George Square. The catering staff were GMWU members and at first agreed to a union request not to work on the lunch, but were then talked round by David Hodge to doing it after all, and it went ahead. Some really crass racist remarks from Hodge didn't help to dampen the outrage (see p.96), and Hodge was expelled from the Labour Group. He held a lunch again the next year.

All these factors, plus the early stages of the UK campaign about Mandela, produced the context in which the Freedom of the City proposal emerged in 1980. Different people claim to have first suggested the idea – David Wiseman and Janey Buchan for two – but whatever the truth there, the idea emerged as a motion from Kelvingrove Constituency Labour Party to the District Labour Party. At our fringe meeting at the STUC this past April, John Brown, Scottish Secretary of the Communications Workers Union, got up and spoke about being Secretary of the District Labour Party at that time, and the need to argue the case there since not everyone was immediately supportive. Our own minutes of August 1980 record that Ian Davidson had asked if our trade union contacts could lobby Labour councillors as the matter passed from the District Labour Party to the Labour Group. At our December meeting it was reported that the Freedom of the City had been formally approved.

At about the same time, the Scottish Area of National Union of Mineworkers (NUMSA) invited Mandela to attend their 1981 Miners Gala in Edinburgh.

Brian's contribution here will take up the rest of the story. I'll just add that contacts with local authorities continued in all sorts of small and unpublicized ways, as well as the big set-piece events, and in 1985 we helped set up the Scottish Committee for Local Authority Action Against Apartheid, for which Brian acted as Secretary. The local authority boycott was made illegal by the Thatcher government, but Councils found other ways of supporting us in the cause of South African freedom, in very public and practical ways, for which we are deeply grateful. The detail of all that, however, would be a whole new discussion.

Metal Anti-Apartheid badge, 1980s,
Glasgow Museums collection PP.2015.64.1121.
Given to Glasgow Museums by the family of
Andy Thomson, 2015.
Image © CSG CIC Glasgow Museums Collection.

Nelson Mandela and the Freedom of the City of Glasgow, 1981–1993: Brian Filling

Glasgow awarded the Freedom of the City to Nelson Mandela on 4 August 1981, the first city in the world to do so. Three other places in Scotland – Aberdeen, Dundee and Midlothian District – also made the award in succeeding years, bringing the total to nine in the UK, before Mandela was released on 11 February 1990.

Edinburgh could never get a two-thirds majority in the Council [to support the awarding of the Freedom of the City to Mandela], which was principally because the Tories would never vote for it. The Labour group, which led the Council in Edinburgh, decided to create a statue, *Woman and Child*, dedicated to the freedom fighters of South Africa. This is in Festival Square in Edinburgh, and was unveiled by Suganya Chetty. Edinburgh did eventually award Mandela the Freedom of the City, in 1998.

The award of Freedom of the City of Glasgow to Nelson Mandela didn't come out of nowhere; the Anti-Apartheid Movement had organized petitions, pickets, boycotts, demonstrations, torch-light processions, conferences, cultural and all kinds of other events prior to this.

It was a long campaign to end apartheid, and often people would say, 'You're never going to manage this. You're never going to win'. The apartheid regime presented itself as invincible and omnipotent, hoping to persuade the world that it was going to be there forever, but the South African people and the worldwide solidarity movement proved it wrong. The campaign also showed how ordinary people can change things.

Some people may think that everybody was in favour of Mandela being given the Freedom of the City; however, that was not the case. The Lord Provost of Glasgow, David Hodge, hosted a lunch for the Apartheid South African Ambassador in 1978, which we picketed. He actually said, 'How can you expect people to come out of the jungle and go into government?' As this was coincident with the negotiations over Zimbabwe's independence it was understood to be a reference to that. Racism was not uncommon. David Hodge was thrown out of the Labour group, but remained as Lord Provost. At the next election, the Labour group came into office and a new Lord Provost, Michael Kelly, was elected. The incident with Hodge had been very embarrassing for the Labour Party, and so a resolution from Kelvingrove CLP [Constituency Labour Party] to compensate for this went all the way up to the Council Labour Group and was then passed by the Council.

I spent some time on the day of the award behind the scenes prior to the official ceremony, trying to persuade the officials that the ANC [African National Congress] Chief Representative should be on the platform at the event. There was a reticence about being too associated with the ANC and the armed struggle in South Africa.

This was understandable, because Mandela was still being described as a terrorist by the Thatcher Tory government and the media.

Alex Ekwueme, the Vice-President of Nigeria, accepted the award on behalf of Mandela in absentia, because he was still imprisoned on Robben Island. There was a lunch after the ceremony and during this the Vice-President said, 'I've been invited by the Anti-Apartheid Movement [AAM] to speak at a meeting this afternoon', and he said, 'Is Brian Filling here? Can I invite people to this meeting?' Vice-President Ekwueme wanted to tell the world, and Britain in particular, why Nigeria had just nationalized British Petroleum (BP). At the AAM meeting he explained that this was because of its busting of UN sanctions against Rhodesia. The meeting also provided a platform for Ruth Mompati, the ANC Chief Representative, who outlined the struggle against apartheid.

Later that day, at a dinner hosted by Ekwueme at the Albany Hotel, I was invited to sit at the top table, as was Ruth Mompati, who was now one of the speakers. Michael Kelly in his speech that night said, 'Now, you need to understand why the South African people have taken up the armed struggle'. Sixteen High Commissioners from across the Commonwealth had attended the Freedom of the City ceremony in the morning, and I think this had impressed Michael and others. Their presence indicated that Glasgow was not isolated, but rather that actually the world was siding with the anti-apartheid struggle. It was the British government which was at odds.

I had known Mike Terry from when he was National Secretary of the National Union of Students, and we had worked together in London on campaigns in the early 1970s. During that period, I got to know a lot of the ANC people in exile. When Mike became Secretary of the Anti-Apartheid Movement in the UK, I became Chair of the Scottish Committee of the Anti-Apartheid Movement, in 1976. So, working with Mike over many years meant that we had a close political relationship.

Following the Freedom of the City being given to Mandela, Mike and I discussed how we could take it forward. One idea we had was to get the UN Special Committee Against Apartheid to invite the Lord Provost to launch a worldwide mayors' petition calling for Mandela's release. Mike discussed the idea with ES Reddy of the UN Special Committee Against Apartheid, and the invitation was made.

Lord Provost Michael Kelly went to the UN in New York and launched the petition. Several thousand mayors from all over the world signed the petition. That put Glasgow on the world stage as the first city to give its Freedom to Nelson Mandela, but it was now much wider than that. We were on a roll!

Kelly's successor as Lord Provost, Bob Gray, was also supportive, and he led a deputation of UK Lord Mayors in all their ermine and gowns and hats to Downing Street in 1984, with a petition calling on [Prime Minister] Mrs Thatcher to support the release of Nelson Mandela.

The next idea was to re-name a street in Glasgow. There were differing views as to which street this should be. Eventually it was agreed to re-name St George's Place, in the centre of Glasgow. This was most appropriate as we often held pickets there. It was where the Apartheid South African Consulate was located, on the fifth floor of the Stock Exchange building. In 1986 St George's Place was re-named Nelson Mandela Place. The nameplate was unveiled by Essop Pahad of the African National Congress.

Metal and plastic Anti-Apartheid badge, produced for the Anti-Apartheid Movement's 'Nelson Mandela: Freedom at 70' campaign in 1988. It was launched for Mandela's 70th birthday, 18 July 1988. Glasgow Museums collection PP.2015.64.1125. Given to Glasgow Museums by the family of Andy Thomson, 2015. Image © CSG CIC Glasgow Museums Collection.

The next big event was on 12 June 1988, when we organized a demonstration from Kelvingrove Park to a huge rally on Glasgow Green. We sent off 25 marchers, each one representing a year of Mandela's life in prison. It was the day after the Wembley Concert calling for Mandela's release at the age of 70, which was televised and watched by millions across the world.

At the rally Oliver Tambo, leader of the African National Congress in exile while Mandela was in prison, was the main speaker. Other speakers included Alan Boesak of the United Democratic Front in South Africa, Bernie Grant MP, Janey Buchan MEP, and Campbell Christie of the STUC.

It was a beautiful day, and the atmosphere was tremendous with some 30,000 people in attendance. The crowd were warmed up by an Angolan band, and when I introduced Oliver Tambo he was met with rapturous applause. The marchers arrived in London for Mandela's birthday on 18 July, and were greeted at a rally in Hyde Park addressed by Archbishop Desmond Tutu.

Mandela was eventually released on 11 February 1990, and we celebrated that evening in Nelson Mandela Place, bringing traffic to a standstill. The apartheid consulate was eventually closed in 1992, so we won that campaign.

Local Authority Action Against Apartheid [which co-ordinated local authority action] decided to invite Mandela to the UK to receive the Freedoms of those nine UK cities which had awarded him this. The ANC proposed that the event should be held in one city, as Nelson was no longer a young man and it was now in the run up to the election. I was appointed to liaise between Mandela's office, the ANC and the nine cities, which I regarded as a great honour. Mandela's office and the ANC were easy to deal with – they wanted him to visit only one place because he should really have been in South Africa campaigning in the run-up to the election. However, trying to get the other cities to agree proved more difficult. Understandably, they all wanted him to come to their city.

Aberdeen was the last to agree [to it being in one city]. This was reasonable, as it had initiated the boycott of South African goods in 1964 and Bob Hughes, an Aberdeen MP, was Chair of the UK Anti-Apartheid Movement. Unfortunately, I had then to tell them that each city was only going to get five minutes with Mandela. Now, five minutes with representatives of each of the nine cities plus moving around would amount to one hour. We didn't think this was the best use of Mandela's time at his age and at this critical time in South African history. Aberdeen then threatened again to pull out of the event, and their Council leader offered to transport Mandela in a helicopter from Glasgow to Aberdeen. We knew that if another city was allowed to have him then all the others would pull out. So, we had to resist that, and Aberdeen eventually agreed to come.

Nelson Mandela came to Glasgow and received the Freedoms of nine UK cities, districts and boroughs at a special ceremony in the City Chambers on 9 October 1993. It was arranged that all the cities would get to meet Mandela separately. This was arranged in Glasgow City Chambers, three cities per room, and each of them was allowed ten delegates. We proposed to put them in alphabetical order, rather than chronologically by date of the awarding of their Freedom of the City. So, Aberdeen was put first. That managed to get them there!

As I said, we were worried about Mandela and this use of his time. However, when he came in and shook the hand of the first woman councillor from Aberdeen he said, 'Thank you so much for coming in this dreadful weather from the Granite City'. I should point out that there was torrential rain that day. Now, we had briefed Mandela, but I don't recall talking about the Granite City.

Mandela then went down the whole line, saying something to each of them individually, and then made an impromptu speech about Aberdeen and its role in the boycott. Afterwards, the leader of Aberdeen City Council apologized for the amount of time I had spent negotiating to get them there and said, 'That was the most wonderful five minutes of my life, thank you so much. I'm glad you persuaded us'. I was able to say, 'When you look at the video it's actually only three and half minutes!'

Mandela made an incredible impression on people in a very, very short time. He turned that one hour of what could have been just a ritualistic shaking of hands into a really memorable event that he clearly enjoyed. That came across to everyone. It was fantastic.

Later, there was a special ceremony in the Banqueting Hall, with invited guests as well as the representatives from the nine cities. Mandela received a rapturous welcome when I introduced him afterwards to a huge crowd in George Square. In his speech he condemned the apartheid regime for its use of a Third Force conducting killings in South Africa to de-rail the elections. Some people think it was a bloodless revolution, but in fact some 10,000 people were killed by proxy by the regime in the years from Mandela's release in 1990 until the election in 1994. This was later confirmed by the Truth and Reconciliation Commission with statements made by those who were responsible.

Next day we held a press conference, very early on the Sunday morning, and invited the editors of newspapers. They were really resistant to come at eight o'clock on a Sunday morning, I can assure you. But they did, and Mandela began the press conference by saying 'Now, rather than me making a speech, I'll answer the questions which will be in your minds, "What is my personal relationship with Winnie and my political relationship with Chief Buthelezi?"' These were the big issues of the day in the media. He answered these questions and then went on to talk about the Third Force in South Africa which was killing thousands of people and potentially jeopardizing the elections there. At the end of the press conference he got a standing ovation from the editors and wonderfully positive news coverage.

At his speech in the Banqueting Hall of the City Chambers he said, 'It's a special privilege to be a guest of this great city of Glasgow. It will always enjoy a distinguished place in the records of the international campaign against apartheid. The people of Glasgow in 1981 were the first in the world to confer on me the Freedom of the City, at a time when I and my comrades were in prison on Robben Island serving life sentences which, in apartheid South Africa, then meant imprisonment until death. Whilst we were physically denied our freedom in the country of our birth, a city 6,000 miles away, and as renowned as Glasgow, refused to accept the legitimacy of the apartheid system and declared us to be free'.

Freedom of the City of Glasgow had a special meaning not only for Nelson Mandela, but also for all the other South African political prisoners. And not just for them but for the African National Congress and the South African people. So, Glasgow is held in special esteem by the people of South Africa. When you go there and talk to people, it's surprising how many people know about this and the impact it had. What began as a modest campaign turned into a mass movement.

Those of you who were there on the day that Mandela visited Glasgow will treasure that, I'm sure, as a memory forever. The African National Congress won the first democratic election in South Africa on 27 April 1994, and I was fortunate to be invited as a guest to the inauguration of Nelson Mandela as President on 10 May 1994 in Pretoria.

Further Resources

Glasgow Caledonian University's Archive Centre

The records of the Scottish Committee of the Anti-Apartheid Movement (AAM) are held at Glasgow Caledonian University's Archive Centre. These records came from Brian Filling and John Nelson, collected and preserved by them in their roles as Chair and Secretary respectively, and document Scotland's role in the fight against apartheid. The main coverage is 1976 to 1994, although some records from the 1960s and early 1970s are also held.

The research strengths of this collection are:
Scottish Anti-Apartheid Movement
Pressure groups and protest movements
South and southern Africa
Racial discrimination and prejudice
Social justice
Human rights
Nelson Mandela/leading African National Congress (ANC) activists
Art and culture in political struggle

To find out more, or to contact us, visit https://www.gcu.ac.uk/archives

Glasgow Museums Resource Centre (GMRC) and Kelvin Hall

Glasgow City Council owns one of the greatest civic museum collections in Europe, containing over one million accessioned objects. Its size and diversity reflect the eclectic Victorian origins of the collections, and over 150 years of collecting across the general subject areas of art, natural history, human history, and transport and technology. The collection is a Recognized Collection of National Significance to Scotland, and includes local labour history, and trade union and protest banners.

GMRC, in Nitshill, is a purpose-built publicly accessible store for Glasgow Museums' collections when they are not on display in the City's 10 museum venues. The main collections stored here are Art and Painting, Arms and Armour, Natural History, Technology and World Cultures. The 17 purpose-built and environmentally controlled storage 'pods' house around one million objects. We offer a wide range of tours, talks and activities for all ages, including school visits and events for families with children.

Kelvin Hall is a unique partnership between Glasgow Life, the University of Glasgow, and the National Library of Scotland, which sees this historic and much-loved venue transformed into an exciting centre of cultural excellence providing access to collections, temporary displays, teaching and research. Glasgow Museums' Social History, Charles Rennie Mackintosh, Archaeology and furniture collections are stored here.

To view objects located at Glasgow Museums Resource Centre or Kelvin Hall, email navigator@glasgowlife.org.uk. Some of the collections may be viewed online at http://collections.glasgowmuseums.com/mwebcgi/mweb

To find out about tours and the activity programme at GMRC, phone 0141 276 9300, email GMRCBookings@glasgowlife.org.uk, or visit https://www.glasgowlife.org.uk/museums/venues/glasgow-museums-resource-centre-gmrc

To find out about tours and the activity programme at Kelvin Hall, visit https://kelvinhall.org.uk/glasgow-museums/

Glasgow Women's Library (GWL)

Glasgow Women's Library is the UK's only Accredited Museum dedicated to women's lives, histories and achievements, with a lending library, archive collections and innovative programmes of public events and learning opportunities. A designated Recognized Collection of National Significance, GWL champions, celebrates and teaches us about how women have shaped lives, families, communities and the country. Women's stories are told through GWL's remarkable collection, documenting their 'everyday' popular domestic and leisurely past times, together with their demands for change in waves of activism that address inequality.

Glasgow Women's Library, 23 Landressy Street, Glasgow G40 1BP
www.womenslibrary.org.uk
Tel: 0141 550 2267
Twitter/Instagram @womenslibrary
Facebook https://www.facebook.com/womenslibrary

The Nelson Mandela Scottish Memorial Foundation

The Nelson Mandela Scottish Memorial Foundation is a charity which exists to raise awareness of apartheid, the anti-apartheid struggle, Mandela's part in that, and his strong links with Scotland. His life and legacy have many lessons for a world still struggling with racial and social injustice. A planned statue in Glasgow's Nelson Mandela Place is a key focus and teaching aid for this, both during the fundraising stage and after completion. Materials for schools have been very successfully piloted, and publication online and in print makes these available to all.

Visit http://mandelascottishmemorial.org for more information.

Scottish Labour History Society

For more details of the Society, see the Foreword on p.1. The Scottish Labour History Society welcomes all interested in the promotion of labour history. Current annual subscription fees for individual members are £15 (waged) and £10 (unwaged), with special fees for organizations available upon request. You can join the Society and subscribe at www.scottishlabourhistorysociety.scot, or by post by contacting S. Maclennan, 0/1, 64 Terregles Ave, Glasgow G41 4LX, Scotland. Further copies of this publication and the following Occasional Publications may also be purchased:

- *Cowie Miners, Polmaise Colliery and the 1984–85 Miners' Strike*, 2017, Steve McGrail with Vicky Patterson
- *John Maclean: The Speech From The Dock*, 2018, Ewan Gibbs and Rory Scothorne (Eds)
- *'Sanny' Sloan: The Miners' MP*, 2020, Esther Davies.

About the Editors

David Featherstone is Reader in Human Geography at the University of Glasgow and has research interests in labour geography and labour history. He is the author of *Solidarity: Hidden Histories and Geographies of Internationalism*, Zed Books, 2012.

Fiona Hayes is Curator of Social History for Glasgow Museums. Her collection areas cover various aspects of Glasgow history from the mid-18th century to the present, including protest movements, popular culture, civic history, topography including photography, home and working life, and women's history. She has written about Glasgow Museums' photographic collections in *Glasgow 1955: Through the Lens* and *1970s Glasgow: Through the Lens* and has also contributed to Glasgow Museums' publications *Introducing Georgian Glasgow – How Glasgow Flourished; Fred A Farrell Glasgow's War Artist* and *Out There – The Open Museum: Pushing the boundaries of museums' potential*. She is a graduate of the University of Edinburgh, with a postgraduate diploma in Museum Studies (specializing in social and industrial history) from the University of Leicester, and is an Associate of the Museums Association.

Helen M Hughes BSc, Dip Cons (Tex), ACR, is a Textile Conservator at Glasgow Museums. She trained at the Textile Conservation Centre, Courtauld Institute, University of London, and has worked on many exhibitions and projects including *Banners of the World* and the STUC centenary exhibition in Kelvingrove; on the Kelvingrove New Century Project; the Burrell Tapestries Project and as a contributor to the accompanying catalogue *Glasgow Museums: Tapestries from the Burrell Collection*, published in conjunction with Philip Wilson Publishers; and on *Banner Tales of Glasgow*.

Isobel McDonald has been a curator of Social History at Glasgow Museums since 2008, with responsibility for the education, toys, sport, health and Home Front collections. Recent exhibitions which she has curated include *Brushes with War* (2018, Kelvingrove Art Gallery and Museum), and *GlaswegAsians* (2017–2020, Scotland Street School Museum). She is the author of *Coming Into View: Eric Watt's photographs of Glasgow*, Glasgow Museums, 2020.

Acknowledgements

We would like to thank everyone who was involved in, attended, or contributed to the events this publication is based on. Many thanks to Carole McCallum and David Ward from the Archive Centre at Glasgow Caledonian University who co-organized the Anti-Apartheid Banners event. Thanks too to the staff and volunteers from Glasgow Women's Library, in particular Dr Adele Patrick and Laura Dolan, for their help and support with the 'Women and the Peace Movement' event in GWL. We would also like to thank Dominic Allan, Johnnie Crossan, William Docherty, Chris Jamieson, Richard Leonard and Helen Watkins for their invaluable contributions to the *Banner Tales* project. The support and encouragement of Diarmaid Kelliher, Ewan Gibbs, Stewart Maclennan and Valerie Wright at the Scottish Labour History Society has been greatly appreciated, and we thank them for their assistance in bringing this to print. Thanks to Jay Bernard for all their work on designing the publication, Jacqui Duffus for taking up the mantle and finalizing the publication for print, Susan Pacitti at Glasgow Museums for her careful preparation of the text, and to Alan Wylie for permission to include his photographs. Finally, many thanks to the contributors for their patience and engagement with the editing process. We hope this publication goes some way to doing their stories and experiences justice.